T0245850

OCTOBER 7

Voices of Survivors and Witnesses

Compiled by Tal Chaika
with Lily Marks

Introduction by Yitzhak Herzog

Foreword by Eric D. Fingerhut

PROSPECTA PRESS

Originally published in Hebrew in January 2024.

Paperback ISBN 978-1-63226-149-6
eBook ISBN 978-1-63226-150-2

Published by Prospecta Press
PO Box 3131
Westport CT 06880

www.prospectapress.com

Book and cover design by Barbara Aronica

For more information, visit https:/www.oct7book.com

Proceeds from the publication of this book will be provided to organizations that support the survivors and their families.

This book was created entirely
voluntarily and as part of a
mission to commemorate the stories of
Hamas's October 7 massacres in Israel
and the war that followed.

We hope and pray for the speedy,
healthy, and safe return of all the
hostages and IDF soldiers.

~

All proceeds from this book
will be donated to the victims and
survivors of the October 7 attack
and the war that followed.

INTRODUCTION

Greetings,

In this work, we are presented with impressions and memories of the tragic events that occurred on Saturday, October 7, a holiday, which turned into a national tragedy unprecedented in its scope.

The sheer scale of the carnage and brutality left many of us in shock and disbelief. Can any of us truly find words to adequately describe such horrors, given their magnitude? This rings particularly true for those who endured those harrowing hours on the killing fields; even if they survived, their souls remain deeply scarred. The turmoil, both personal and national, will continue to haunt us for years to come.

An act of commemoration and remembrance seems natural in these tragic circumstances. This is, of course, a monument for our beloved brothers and sisters whose lives were cruelly snatched away on that fateful day but will be in our hearts forever, and for all who were hurt in body and soul.

But preserving the memory, precisely because it is terrible and unfathomable, has an added value: It ensures that the truth of what transpired on that dark day is universally acknowledged and understood, preventing any attempt to deny what happened there, on that black day. That all will recognize the power of carnage and evil. That it is clear who is the aggressor—cruel, bloodthirsty, and lacking in humanity—and who clings to life, in goodness and joy, but is butchered and slaughtered. That we see the difference between those who are cruel, bloodthirsty, and devoid of humanity—and the victims, who were brutally slain in the middle of a party or home in front of their family or were mercilessly abducted into darkness.

We are a nation that remembers, bearing a long, complex, and storied past. As one of Israel's eminent figures once stated, there is redemption in remembrance itself. The sights and experiences of that day are indeed unbearably painful, but becoming acquainted with them—and with the extraordinary men and women we lost, as well as the many heroes who fought and continue to fight with courage, many of whom have also fallen—is crucial. Their stories, along with those of thousands of our beloved people who have rallied to the cause both on the front lines and at home, inspire us to cherish life and all that we have, fostering our resolve to rebuild and strengthen our nation.

Therefore, I extend my gratitude for your initiative and its successful realization, which honors the ancient biblical command "so that your generations may know," perpetuating the memory of our loved ones, the fallen and the murdered, in the history of the State of Israel and the Jewish people.

With sincere appreciation and gratitude,

—Yitzhak Herzog

President

12th of Tevet, 5784

December 24, 2023

FOREWORD

For every one of the three generations since the Holocaust, we've made the same promise over and over: Never Again. And then came October 7. We realized, with inexpressible shock and sorrow, that for one day, it had indeed happened again: a catastrophe on the level of the worst days of the Shoah, the Crusades, and all the tragedies of Jewish history.

Moreover, the largest loss of life in Israel since the founding of the Jewish State happened on Simchat Torah. It happened on Shabbat. It happened on a day of rejoicing turned into unimaginable horror.

Those of us who grew up in an America in which antisemitism had largely receded into the background have experienced a true Golden Age of Jewish life. We are leaders in business, government, the arts, academia, science, and medicine. One simply cannot imagine American society without the contributions of American Jewry.

And we have experienced with joy and pride, and supported with our hearts and resources, the birth and growth of the State of Israel. A strong and vibrant Jewish state, alongside a strong and vibrant Jewish Diaspora—this is our story!

So it is perhaps understandable that the shock of October 7 has caused such emotional trauma to the entire Jewish people. The personal loss is beyond painful, but so is the emotional loss of being plunged from our twenty-first century Jewish existence into the life of so many generations of our people who knew what it was like to be outcast, hunted, and scared for our lives.

There will be many efforts to memorialize October 7. This book is important both as one of the first and because it helps us capture and not forget some of the raw emotions we are experiencing. A mix of extraordinarily moving poetry, eulogies, and other testimonials, it presents ordinary Israelis grappling with unbearable sadness and grief, excruciating survivor guilt, and an indomitable need to bear witness to their loved ones' compassion, selflessness in the face of mortal danger, and incredible acts of heroism.

The authors don't shy away from describing the violent deaths of their family members and friends at the hands of the terrorists, or recalling the surreal, heartbreaking experience of seeing them dragged into captivity. It's one of the hardest books I've ever had to read, but one of the most necessary. Together with trips to the sites of the attack itself and essential projects like the Nova music festival exhibit, which is now touring America, this book helps us comprehend what happened on a day that will, like the destruction of the temples in Jerusalem, reverberate down the ages of Jewish history.

Like the Six-Day War, October 7 also woke many in North American Jewish life from a time of casual connection to Jewish communal life as just one of many great opportunities in America to a deep desire for participation and relevance in this moment in history.

Indeed, as soon as we learned of the terrorist attack, we in our Jewish communities went into overdrive, raising hundreds of millions of dollars in a matter of days to provide humanitarian aid, organizing hundreds of rallies across the continent, mobilizing government officials and faith leaders, and everyone with influence to support Israel and help the Israeli people. The energy has not dissipated, even as the months have gone on.

The stories in this book are a potent reminder of why we are continuing to support Israel in unprecedented ways, even as we cope with the extraordinary antisemitic and anti-Israel fallout from October 7—the anti-Israel protests that have overwhelmed our college campuses, government meetings, and even our public and private schools. The massive rally for Israel that we held in Washington, DC, just a month after the terrorist attack, which drew over a quarter million people, was compared by some to what happened at the foot of Mount Sinai, the last time that so many Jews gathered in a common cause.

But no matter what happens, we in the North American Jewish community will be there for our brothers and sisters in Israel with a mighty hand and an outstretched arm. That's what being a Jew means and that is our sacred vow, now and forever.

—The Honorable Eric D. Fingerhut,
President and CEO of the Jewish
Federations of North America

OCTOBER 7

Yair Elitzur
Since Everything Changed

Time doesn't stop for anyone
And I barely scratched a piece
of deep sadness and loss.
A month has already passed
And a few more days
Since everything has changed
Nothing will be the same again
The heart does not want
cannot understand
A Jewish soul is crying.
Any person kidnapped
is my brother.
Everyone who died
died in me too.
October seventh
is not a date
It's a bottomless pit
With no way out
It is impossible to digest
impossible to contain
It's even hard to write
Even after a month has already passed.
Any person kidnapped
is my brother
All that died
died in me too.

~

Guy Katzovich

The Establishment and Management of a Citizens' War Room While Being in Reserve

Three and a half weeks since the Black Saturday.

1

On October 8, I realized that I'd been frozen on the couch for the past twenty-four hours. Waiting to be called to reserve duty and scrolling relentlessly through the horrors and the Telegram updates. I called my dear friend Nimrod Arnin, one of the organizers of the Nova party where many had been murdered, raped, and kidnapped. I was happy to see that he picked up even with the trauma he went through and was still going through.

We both agreed to arrive at the offices in central Tel Aviv, and we founded what would become the official war room: we went through the ticketing system of the party, and we went over (manually) thousands of correspondences between the production team and some of the participants and their loved ones. Together we built a reliable and deterministic statistical database that today is being used by all the war rooms and the government bodies that are dealing with the missing persons.

We "enriched" the information we gathered with geographic locations (some by going over the correspondences and some by using various technological tools). After the information was transferred to operational forces in the field, dozens of missing persons were tracked through it, and the status of others became clear.

2

In the following days, this sacred operation was transferred to the government bodies and bigger war rooms that were dealing with it, and we, in our high-tech war room, moved on to raising money and mobilizing it to the forces in the field. In just a few days we raised over a million NIS (all of it from small donations from the public, and from a substantial fundraiser organized by my partner, Yair Vardi, with the foundation's investors and other friends in California).

Together we transferred over twenty-one thousand items of equipment to over two hundred units in the field. These days we continue this laborious work, led by dozens of volunteers and hundreds of movers and messengers.

3

In the last few days, we launched together with the "diners" community (a community of young Israeli leaders) the Strong Together campaign, for a strong home front. Imagine some sort of a virtual school and community, but for grownups. Every day we have lessons and get-togethers in every subject that could help us get through this time: from how to manage our households and businesses during wartime to an analysis of the geopolitical situation from different angles, and of course tools and lessons on how to reduce stress—psychology sessions with psychiatrists, therapists, and other teachers.

We have only just begun, and there is more content coming.

4

On this subject we'll release further explanations in a different post in the future, when the time is right: over the last month we invested in nine new preseed companies in Fusion VC.

And after two weeks of almost no activity, we're going back to meeting new companies starting next week. We also invested in other portfolio companies that are recruiting their second funding and investment rounds. We will say more about this, hopefully soon, and about the support we're giving the portfolio, at the proper time.

5

And in between there were also the reserves, yes.

I could have written here about broken conceptions, about the civilian security that has cracked, and too many things we need to fix here after the war. But between being drafted to the reserves, starting the civilian war room, and trying to do "business as usual" in emergency times, I think it's better to choose the good, and the action that is happening across genders and nationalities in Israeli society right now.

To conclude I want to thank Nimrod Arnin (Nimi), Dor Rahamim, Yotam Ben-Halifa, Raz Malka, and the rest of the Nova people who opened their hearts and database to us to save lives, literally.

Thanks to all the war room people who are working day and night for good things to happen: Nir Na'amani, Guy Liobovich, Sivan Raznikov, Guy Kimchi, Roee Zur, Gal Brazily, Eyal Daniel, Lior Avishar, Amitai Razon, Miri Zuk, Eran Farkash, Alon Malzov, Eylon Sa'adon, Noa Eylon, Yoval Karmi, Shani Zansko, Eyal Blizer, Hila Katz, Tal Havusha Barak, Saar Litman, Ido Perry, Eldar Solomon, Gefen Rotem Yamin, and many more that I must have forgotten (I ask for your forgiveness).

And thanks to Dekel Ya'akobovich for Strong Together, to Yoav Vilner, Noa Zilberman, Yaniv Rivlin, Tom Bar-Av, and

Yahli Sa'ar for all the support in the war room, and to Itay Rimmer for getting to know you.

And thanks to my partner, family, and friends who support me in this time.

"And there is a thing where we'll turn it all for good."

~

Yuval Siman–Tov
Reborn

The picture: a moment before.

One hundred twenty hours have passed since the moment I was reborn.

From the moment I ended my life and received it back.

After so many thoughts, crying, nightmares, pain, I decide to tell the story. Tell so I can give some hint of the blackest day I experienced, we experienced, are experiencing.

We leave my house in Rehovot for the party; Tamir Leshetz and Ron Weinberg first come in to pee at my place and take the fishing rod out of the car. After all, it is a fifty-minute drive at 1:00 in the morning, and it's not easy.

1:55—Turn right at the "Reim" sign toward a huge area, dozens of cars, thousands of people.

We pass the strict security check, and from there we go to sit with our friends, along with twenty other people.

We go to the bathroom before dancing, and I meet my friend Matan Zanati. Sooo many laughs. How I love this guy. We spend a long time full of fun, taking pictures and going to dance together. He's from Dimona and we were together almost our entire military service, so this is a really unique opportunity to meet. We laugh about how with our luck there will be rockets. I go back to the kanta.

Ron, Tamir, and I are super happy. Although it's full of people, it's so much fun. Dancing and sitting and dancing again and sitting again.

It's 6:10. Ron decides to stay outside to dance. It's his first nature party, and after I gave him my earplugs, he must have been having a great time. I understand.

Tamir and I sit down, waiting for the sun to rise at 6:30, like everyone else, I guess. Talking, laughing. Tamir is the greatest friend, and every moment with him is pure happiness.

6:30. We begin to see flashes of light in the sky. Another five, another ten. I look at my phone—alarms in the center of Israel. What a bummer. The party's done.

We lie down on the ground, the music stops, and the DJ says, "There are sirens, Red Alert—lie down on the ground."

Ron lies farther down on the ground, and Tamir and I don't understand what's happening. Thousands of people are running everywhere. Real panic. A loud boom next to us, another boom and another one.

The policeman comes up and announces, "Dear friends, you only have fifteen seconds. Run away from here as fast as possible."

People next to me are wondering to themselves, is running away the right move? Each time in our lives that this has happened, we were taught that we shouldn't run away at such a moment, we should stay. The cops insist.

Ron runs toward us, I put on a sweatshirt, Tamir the hat, Ron the shirt.

We fold everything quickly; next to us people are going mad, everybody's stressed, some are screaming. We all let our family know that everything's fine despite the nonstop booms, the rockets falling near us, and the sirens. We start running to the car. None of us can imagine the nightmare that has started from that moment, and continues for the rest of our lives.

On the way to the car, the situation is chaotic. People are running to cars that don't belong to them, cars are backing up on people, people are crying. We get to the car quickly, load the luggage. Ron asks me to sit in front, he sits in back, and we start driving. Standing still in the huge line of cars, and we haven't even reached the driveway yet. Two minutes. No progress. I see an escape lane between cars in the last parking lane. I tell Tamir to drive that way. He hesitates a little because the car will be damaged, and I can understand him—after all, it's a Nissan from 2009.

We decide to go for it. The car bounces between the hills and we reach the road, the road of death, the road of murder, road 232. Two police cars block the road heading north. We're going crazy, why, how? Most of the country is going north! We ask—and they immediately scream at us to start driving in the other direction.

6:49—we start the ride south. Tamir shouts to call the police but they're not answering. What does it mean that they're not answering? It's the police. No answer. Again and again. We continue driving south. Kfir, who's in Thailand, texts me nonstop that we are making a mistake and must stop at a migunit (roadside bomb shelter).

I agree with him, this is what each and every one of us was taught to do. When the missiles don't stop and land not far from you, and there are sirens at any given moment, you stop, you wait. You don't drive. But some instinct stops me, stops me from stopping.

Every time we drive past a migunit, I tell Tamir to stop and he doesn't stop. Eventually, he asks me whether he should stop, and I have a change of heart, I tell him to continue. We pass dozens of roadside bomb shelters. In the meantime, Ron calls his friend Johnny, telling him that he can't believe this is how his first nature party ended, how much he enjoyed it, and how crazy this is. I'm on Waze, and I see that we are approaching the south of the Gaza Envelope at 120 kmh, light years away from Rehovot; we've been driving for ten minutes. Waze says to just turn around, there's no other option.

I look back—an empty road. I look ahead—an empty road. No one is driving behind us. How strange. There were thousands of people at the party; where did they run off to? Surely this means they opened the road north. I knew we had to wait. I say this to Tamir and Ron, and they agree. We go into one of the kibbutzim, turn around, and start heading back north. Driving and driving. Five minutes later, a white Toyota Corolla police car passes us at high speed. I calm down, I tell my sister, my friends, and my girlfriend that everything is fine with us and we are on our way home. And suddenly the police car starts slowing down: 120, 90, 60, 30. Tamir gets angry. We have to get out of there, the missiles aren't stopping, and I'm starting to get restless again. We're all debating in the car. We decide to cross the line and change lanes for our lives.

We honk twice and start going. Suddenly the policeman puts his hand out of the window and bangs on the door. We stop next to him, I open the window, I look at his terrified face, and he screams, "Terrorists are coming toward you! Turn around!"

I say to him, "What?"

He screams out again, "Terrorists!"

Tamir reverses quickly, and I look to the right: three motorcyclists with weapons are a few hundred meters away from us. As we turn back south, I'm shaking with fear. Ron behind me doesn't understand what's going on, and me and Tamir are holding hands. I call the police again—7:05—no answer. We no longer see the policeman behind us, and we've managed to drive far away from the motorcyclists. Maybe we're safe?

After two minutes, our hands still clasped together, Tamir

notices some people in the distance, we don't know who. He asks me, "Are those terrorists?" I tell him I have no idea, and he shouts, "Terrorists!"

Suddenly—life stops. From the other side of the road arrive eight motorcycles, on each of which is a driver and a shooter, two ATVs, and a van with a submachine gun.

We lower our heads, and from a fifty-meter range they move ahead, shooting and puncturing our vehicle. I have my head down, completely accepting death. After only one second, Ron agonizingly tells us that he's dead. No, bro, I'm dead. I will never forget this feeling for my entire life. Me and Tamir still have our heads down; Tamir is looking at him.

Hundreds of bullets are fired at the car, hundreds. Metal noises, glass explosions, all the windows are exploding, the padding above my head is being shot with bullets. It feels like an eternity: the seconds before death.

Suddenly we raise our heads. The road is clear in front of us; there are no mirrors to check for terrorists behind us. I scream for Tamir to go. Ron groans in pain. And then the news. Tamir says that the car is not working. I ask what that means and he explains. No brakes, no gas, no steering wheel. Nothing. So I accept death for the second time.

Switch to parking, lift the handbrake. Slide and squeak to the side up to the edge of the road.

And this is the terrible moment. Going out to that battlefield, to the road of death. I will never forget that moment.

I look in the back window. Ron is just dying. He is bleeding to death and helpless. We release the belt, get out from both sides of the vehicle. From the north: the terrorist squad.

Coming back toward us are six motorcycles this time, and a van with one submachine gun. We see them making their way toward us, sniping at the other cars on the way, people screaming and crashing their cars. From the south, five more motorcycles are coming toward us, fast. We look toward the fields: two terrorists continue to shoot at the vehicle.

And that's how it is. Under fire. In my time in the IDF, I was in an intelligence combat unit, but never a battlefield. Tamir and I are standing on the road, and the gunfire starts again. Shooting from everywhere at us. Dozens of bullets whistling from all sides. From all sides. From all sides.

We begin our run into the fields but we feel like sitting ducks. A minute of running with nonstop shooting.

Accepting death completely. Life passes before our eyes. It's not a cliché if I'm honest. This is the truth and this is life.

Tamir shouts at me and I shout at him. He runs faster than me. I understand that if I don't fall now, they will catch me. They are chasing me from everywhere. I fall on the floor, pretending to be dead. Tamir screams at me with all his might and sees me disappear. I see the terrorists approaching him and shooting in his direction. He disappears. As far as I know, he has been killed.

I pretend to be dead. And Tamir disappears. And I'm alone. Tamir and Ron are not with me and I'm alone in the world, completely alone.

And the terrorist comes near me, twenty meters away, looks at me, and with the help of a higher power—and only a higher power—he does not kill me. He doesn't shoot me. He does not fucking shoot me.

He continues back to the road.

I look at the road. More and more motorcycles, more and more shooting, screaming at high decibels.

I lie on the ground, completely playing dead. After a few

minutes, I pick up my phone and send a message to whoever possible, wherever I can. I send my location and pray.

Crying, wow, how much I cry. Everyone is dead and I'm alive.

And then it comes, the third time. The third time I die. I feel a very sharp pain in my back, a brutal pain. So I check and take off the sweatshirt. A pink sweatshirt. But not anymore. The sweatshirt is full of blood. All of it, all of it, all of it.

I take off my shirt—two holes in the center of the back, and the shirt is full of blood.

I think this is the end, and this time for real. I put my head back on the ground. At this moment you don't pray for anything. You're mostly hollow. Hollow from everything.

And I wait a few more minutes and get up, breathe heavily, and call my girlfriend, Noa. It is the most difficult call ever—you must have seen it on TV; imagine the exact same call.

She begs for me to live, and I breathe heavily and feel, again, that this is the end.

I reach the inner road, pass the greenhouses, take off the bloody sweatshirt there, and call my sister to tell her. Our parents are abroad and she is all I have left here.

The friends chatter and write everywhere that we are going through this together. I don't believe it, but I want to believe it so much.

A car passes by, opens the window. I shout, "Please help me, I'm about to die, I need you to take me from here." And he continues to drive. He thinks I'm a terrorist.

And I shout to him again from afar, and he comes back.

He gets out of the car, pulls out his weapon, cocks it, aims it at my head. He asks me, "What's your name?"

I tell him, "Yuval from Rehovot." I approach him, begging, and he aims the gun closer at my head. He puts me in the car.

Exactly a nine-second journey. He drops me off at a migunit.

I stagger toward it. There is a foreign worker and me. A fifty-year-old guy runs toward us, covered in blood, and shouts that they shot his entire family and they are all dead. I'm just torn and understand the evil that occurred. We're probably done for. I hug him and ask him to check my back.

Two holes from large shrapnel. One from a large shot and one medium. I take the potentially unwise step of allowing him to pry the two pieces of shrapnel from my back. He presses my blood-soaked shirt on the wounds.

I'm screaming in pain but maybe not in pain? I don't know.

We're there for thirty-five minutes, seeing more terrorists in the distance and shooting. Barely breathing.

The bleeding stops.

There are no soldiers, no MDA, no police.

And then he arrives. Erez Gozan. Yogev, my beloved friend, sent him to me to take me to his bomb shelter at his home in the Yesha settlement.

I get there and hide in the bomb shelter with them, and I am screaming, and screaming, and screaming.

8:30—I'm at their place. For two hours I was on the battlefield running between shots. Hundreds of shots; submachine guns; guns; killers.

Then Tamir calls. That's when I think I really understand. That I'm really alive. When Tamir tells me that I am alive and I tell him that he is alive.

It turns out that he took a completely different path, and in the end he was only two hundred meters from me. I've found my friend, my hero. We both cry our eyes out over Ron who was killed beside us, behind us.

And this is how my next twenty-four hours go. Screaming, nonstop crying, terrorists in the village, bombs. Tremendous pain in the body, but they are probably nothing compared to the pain and fear in the soul. There is no way to describe those twenty-four hours that are more than an eternity.

We try escaping in every way possible without success.

With a full day of efforts from my sister, my girlfriend, all my friends and relatives—we manage to get out.

A private car drives us to the place where my uncle is, and from there we run away to Assaf Harofeh (a hospital).

And I think it is over. And then it comes. Matan Zanati, my friend from service, was also killed. The tragedy doesn't end. The heart is torn in two. So many experiences together, so many conversations together, so much life together, my beloved friend. Yesterday, the members of the squad (from the army) sat together, and our lips raised hymns of love for you, hymns of longing. I am sure that your sweet smile will remain in front of my eyes for the rest of my life. Dancing with you on the dance floor that evening was the last moment of happiness together, brother. What do I have to say beyond that, my brother, what more is there to say.

And ever since then I have been in the same situation. I cry, I sleep a little, and mostly I think. How did I survive? Why me? How out of hundreds of bullets did I manage to get out alive? How was the battlefield I was in, where dozens of terrorists from different places were aiming at me, how was this battlefield real? And here I finish writing and continue to think. Sitting here, with dozens of people who were saved, in the healing space at Beit Yitzhak. In the safest place possible. Talking, breathing, appreciating every moment I'm alive.

And I'm alive. I'm alive. At the age of ten I was in an accident in which I thought I was dying, and I screamed when I got out of there that I was alive. And here I am screaming again. I'm alive. I can live and I want to live. And here I was reborn.

July 7, 2000, I was born.

October 7, 2023, I was reborn.

How do we continue from here? What do we choose?

I actually feel like I know. I want to live for people. Live for the world and not for myself. Live for the world as I have done so far. To concentrate on my nonprofit, JESTA, the place I established for the world, and I want to give more and more to it.

I for sure do not feel like a hero. I feel that we survived. We really survived. But without Ron.

Our beloved late Ron Weinberg was left behind. The man with the smile, the charisma. Love at first sight.

Your funeral was the most spiritual moment ever. Really spiritual. Escorting the coffin in Kibbutz Ein HaShofet, crying on Tamir's shoulders. Thoughts about you, thoughts about how everything could have been different.

Matan and Ron, I will live for you. On my life. All my life.

Tamir, you are my soulmate. I know you don't know I wrote this, but you are everything to me.

Suddenly you realize how everything is nonsense. It is only people, only love, only togetherness. I always believed it but this time more than ever.

Thank you to my girlfriend, my partner for life, who was there for me in every moment and experienced everything with me.

To my amazing sister who showed me the light of life in the darkness of death. To my best friends who saved my life. To everyone who was there with me. Really, thank you. I owe my life to too many people and I only have one life. So I hope you understand.

Tamir, I love you so much. I love you so much. You are everything to me. We are together forever.

You are my hero and I am yours. Unfortunately, no one helped us, not the police, not MDA, and not the hospital.

But it is me and you against the world, together with the amazing people who surround us.

You are my whole life. Thank you for being alive. I'm going through this with you. And crying with you. And hurting with you.

~

The Zionist Leadership Fund
Without Waking the Family

Superintendent Shifra Buchris, forty-five years old, from Merhav Am.

On the morning of Saturday, October 7, Superintendent Shifra Buchris, an officer in the Border Police in the southern region, woke up in her home to a phone call that sent the entire South Border Police unit to Be'er Sheva.

She got up, got ready quickly, and left without waking the family.

On her way, she received a report about an officer wounded in Re'im and decided on her own to go there.

At high speed, she entered into the noisy killing ravine of the Nova party with her team: she and three other policemen in two private cars.

Survivors of the party, almost all of them wounded to varying degrees, sent their families by phone the locations of the hiding places where they hid in the field. The families turned them over to the police, who turned them over to Buchris.

When Buchris and her policemen arrived at a given location, usually a bush, a pit, or behind a tree, Buchris called out loud, "We are the Border Police, we've come to rescue you." She would then load as many of them as possible into the two small vehicles and drive off with them through the road of death between the site of the massacre in Re'im and the collection station of the ambulances at the gas station in Urim.

The road was strewn with punctured, overturned cars; terrorist vans; pools of blood; and countless bodies.

"In the back seat of my Kia, which is made for three people, I usually loaded seven," she explains in retrospect with the shy smile of a policewoman who's violated traffic laws. "I had my M16 with the barrel out in one direction, and Baruch, my policeman, with the gun out in the other direction."

Throughout the day, the entire area was surrounded by a clear and tangible danger of death.

Bursts of gunfire, the sharp buzzing of bullets near the ear, explosions of anti-tank missiles and RPGs, billowing columns of smoke, and ecstatic shouts in Arabic accompanied the "Shifra Team" in the mission initiated by the commander.

They ran to the inferno like the sea, constantly proactively engaging and moving toward the locations sent by the survivors from their phones.

Thus, for over eleven consecutive hours, the Shifra Team made its way back and forth from the evacuation station in Urim to the site of the massacre in Re'im.

The Kia left empty, came back full, left empty again for the inside of the shadow of death, and returned full again . . .

And again, countless times.

The number of lives that Shifra's team was able to save is close to a hundred.

Also, on the way, eleven terrorists were immediately investigated in the field.

What brings a woman like Shifra Buchris, a mother of ten children, to choose of her own accord to repeatedly enter into a clear and immediate danger to her life, for hours on end?

Why is the life of the young people she saved from the party worth more than her own life?

This is the Israeli comradery, the covenant of Jewish destiny, brotherhood, and belief in selfless righteousness, which are the superpower of Zionism.

"I thought about other mothers who want their children back home safely," she says in retrospect.

"I had one thought the whole time. How do we save as many as possible, as many as possible. I had no fear. I knew everything would be okay."

~

Tohar Hava Pappenheim
Sun and Moon—Loop

Waking up each morning with eyes swollen from crying and lack of sleep with a wish that today will be different from yesterday.

That today might bring new and happy news with it, that the long-awaited and exciting phone call will finally arrive. "We are bringing her back to you," they will promise from the other side, and tears of joy and screams of excitement will break out of me like boiling lava.

I raise my eyes to the sky, praying a spontaneous prayer from my guts, from the depths of my soul, begging. I promise to be different, to be better, and only for her.

I take the coffee out of the cupboard, go to the fridge, pour the hot water into a cup, sit down heavily in the dining area, look down at the floor, and bring the coffee cup to my mouth, the bland taste filling my mouth. Every sip stings; every drop of liquid that goes down my throat burns.

She's not here.

What does she drink? What does she eat? How does she manage to fall asleep at night? Is she cold? Does she bathe? Is she injured? And what about her regular medications? What if she is being abused and she is in pain? Tossed like an unwanted object into a corner, trembling with fear and agony, her body defiled, her entire being degraded to dust?

Suddenly the phone rings. Someone asks what's going on and if I need help. I take a deep breath before answering and then heave an earth-shattering sigh, a sigh that only a shattered heart can utter. They understand.

The sun is shining; the birds are chirping in the treetops; cars, buses, vans, and motorcycles are on the road; children's laughter can be heard from the yard next door; the grocer is selling his goods; and the restaurants and cafés are open; but everything is for appearance. This is the superficiality of the world. Internally it feels like a huge black cloud of death covers everything and threatens to bury life and the sun.

They come to help, to voice words of hope and encouragement, and words of ardent faith and confidence in Hashem, confidence in the country, confidence in the power of the people. They come to clean, tidy up, call this person and that one, raise their voices, get angry at politicians, publish endless posts on social networks, put up posters with her portrait wherever possible. They wrap their arms around me, hug me, stroke my head, and comfort me. I imagine myself to be a robot whose movements are controlled automatically and without stopping. I go to an interview in the studio, answer questions on the phone, tell stories, share presently, but I am absent. Breathe and die.

Sitting on a chair surrounded by people, I look to the side and see a furry cat in the yard, and at this sight she rises inside me like a huge wave. How much she loved cats and cared for them, from the abandoned to the most injured. Her heart is as white as snow, a heart rising and overflowing with goodness, a gentleness of soul like no other.

I take a picture and send it to her WhatsApp. They ask a question, I answer, they talk about what Netanyahu said and how Hamas replied to him, but I look at the screen hoping to see that maybe the one tick has been replaced by two blue ticks; will she suddenly type? Write to me, "Mom? I'm fine, don't worry about me, I'll be home soon, big hug." I zoom in on her WhatsApp profile picture. What a radiant smile, how bright her eyes are, how clueless she is about the fire-breathing devil that lurks for her.

Lunch is getting stuck in the throat, a meatball and some rice; the food is soft but every grain and crumb feels hard to swallow, like a stone. My child's hugs succeed in comforting and penetrating the skin and flesh, like a plaster on an aching heart.

A difficult thought creeps in. I try to get rid of it in favor of a better thought. *I wonder if she is talking to anyone? Are there other hostages around her? Does she know how much effort is being invested here for her to return? Does this give her hope?*

And maybe she's getting along and she's being treated okay. The light breaks through me; maybe it's getting closer. And maybe they will take pity on her and release her in the next round. Hope and despair combine inside of me.

Then the sun sets, and the inner and outer darkness merge into an all-consuming darkness. The days pass and the time flies, and the times are like they never were, like one day that has stretched like a long and never-ending rope from that horrible Shabbat and reached this point.

I go to her room, looking at the bookcase that is gathering dust, at the book that is on the dresser, at the red lipstick that is on the table. I look up at her picture on the wall. Look into her eyes and promise: "All my life I will wait for you, until you come back. It will be soon, I feel it, my love, I feel it, maybe even tomorrow morning."

I go to bed, muttering good night to my man; he doesn't recognize his soul, and I don't recognize mine. Both of us are sailing in the terrifying sea of darkness, occasionally with beams of light around us.

I cry into the pillow and fall asleep, until the next day comes.

+ + +

Dedicated to the parents of the hostages who are in Gaza and the parents of those who are missing. Parents whose days are not days and whose nights are not nights. May Hashem put an end to the terrible and continuous nightmare that you are living, and may a cure for your pain soon arrive in the form of your loved one home, as safe and sound as possible. Praying for the unification of hearts right now, and if not right now then tomorrow.

~

Romi Barashi
Life Keeps Running

My name is Romi Barashi, and I am another who was in the massacre in Re'im. It was exactly as it sounds: a massacre.

I ran for my life, shots passed me by, my friends were murdered, burned, and kidnapped.

The whole world needs to know what we've been through.

A group of terrorists planned deliberately to murder innocent people whose only sin was to enjoy and celebrate the life that was then taken from them.

I ran for my life for ten kilometers, shaking with fear, unable to look back; and in the end I was saved by a miracle and ingenuity.

For four hours there was no protection for us, four hours of a continuous nightmare.

The next day, I got a message to get to reserve service, and of course I said yes, but not with a whole heart. I served as an officer and gave an extra year to the country, and at that moment there was no one there for me, for those combat soldiers in the outposts, for those police officers, for the citizens of the Gaza Envelope, for all of us.

I say to you, the political and military ranks: don't let any more citizens feel what we experienced.

There is no other option than to destroy Hamas; these are people who have no place in this world.

They invaded and conquered settlements on bicycles; robbed people of their loved ones, their families; continuously murdered, kidnapped, abused; and in the end also laughed at us. What happened to us, the State of Israel? This is a hotbed of terrorists, a ticking time bomb that will forever want to eliminate us.

I will come to serve because we have no other home, but this time the mistake you made for years you have to correct, in honor of all the families that were destroyed and all those combat soldiers who defended our home with their bodies.

~

Elyasaf Ezra
2:34 in the Morning

The time is 2:34 in the morning.

I don't know how many people will read this post, if any. But I just returned from the funeral of an IDF soldier, the late staff sergeant Roei Wolf. I couldn't wait till the morning to tell the story.

The family asked us to come, so I went. When I drove, my concern was not whether there would be a minyan or not, but whether there would be parking or not. I know my people, and my people don't care that it's on short notice, my people don't care that it's 12:00 a.m., my people care about paying their last respects to a hero of our nation.

All the roads were empty, except for one road, the road that leads to the cemetery. When I arrived, my fear was realized: there was no parking. There was a car in every alley, on every sidewalk, every square meter. All the streets surrounding the cemetery were jammed with parked cars blocking cars blocking other cars. I've never been happier not finding parking.

Thousands of people, thousands upon thousands, came to pay their last respects to Roei Wolf. At the entrance to the cemetery, there was a jam. Thousands entered and thousands did not, because there was no room. People climbed the walls to see his mother, who read the eulogy and said that she had wanted to break his leg so that he wouldn't go to Gaza, but he, even with a broken leg, would have entered, because his blood is not red, but blue and white.

The people of Israel, even with a broken leg, would come to your funeral, Roei.

At your funeral there were all kinds of people: right-wing, left-wing, religious, secular, the whole ensemble. People cried over you. People cried because of the person you were. Of the warrior you were. Of the hero you were. People cried tears of gratitude. People who had never met you, and the first time they met you was after your death, at your funeral.

At the exit of the funeral, there were ultra-Orthodox people with carts full of bottles of water. They gave them to the passersby, to wipe away the tears that were stuck in their throats.

Only in our country, thousands will come to the funeral of a person they have never met.

Only in our country, thousands will cry for a person they have never met.

They didn't know you, but they loved you so much.

I love you so much, Roei.

In your death, you commanded us unity.

~

Shye Weinstein
Surviving Supernova

My name is Shye Weinstein and I am twenty-six years old, from Toronto, Canada, and I am a photographer.

On April 27, 2023, I went to Israel for a planned thirty-day vacation to see my extended family.

Two weeks in, I decided I wouldn't come home. I stayed and made aliyah.

September comes around and my cousin's friend Raz comes over and shares with us about "Sukkot Supernova," the Supernova music festival. It's going to be amazing, huge, the best DJs! We gotta be there!

Right away we're planning and trying to coordinate people. No rush, taking our time with it. I'm hesitant at first, uncertain if I want to go. My conception of a music festival is dirty, gross, lots of people bumping into each other, no toilets, and no food. That was my idea of what a music festival entails, but Supernova turned out to be far better than what I'd imagined.

As I said, initially I was hesitant, but eventually a very dear friend of mine, who I had feelings for, told me she was interested in the festival. So about a day or two before the festival, we bought our tickets together.

Attending the festival was my cousin Mordecai, his girlfriend (now fiancée) Tamara, Yael, Ellie, Dor, Barak, Almog, and myself. Barak and Almog were already at the festival before we arrived to pick out a spot for us.

The night of October 6, we were at a friend's birthday party and from there we went to the festival. Dor and I together, Mordecai and the girls in another car.

Driving to the festival it was late at night, we arrived around 2 a.m. stopping for water at Kfar Aza gas station.

As we headed to the festival ground I found myself growing more and more eager.

Driving up the dirt path we saw the lights shining over the fence and through the trees. Music and heavy bass flowed through the air. We saw all the cars in the parking lot. The festival had a capacity of 4,000 so you need parking for 2,000.

We saw all of the people lined up ready to enter. Dor and I brought out our belongings and joined my cousin and the girls in line, got our wrist bands, got our bags checked, and entered the festival ground.

Now entering the festival ground, you have to walk through the camp area to get to the fun.

We entered the campground through the trees adjacent to the festival ground and we saw among all the trees people sitting with their friends, on chairs, hammocks, smoking, drinking, laughing, joking around, hugging, kissing. It was an incredibly welcoming and positive environment, nobody wasn't having fun. If somebody wasn't having fun they were likely taking a nap.

We made it to our friends, Barak and Almog, who were chilling and waiting for us. We said our hellos and got settled in, got our stuff unpacked and got comfortable. Once we were ready to go, we all took a half pill of ecstasy and added some MDMA to our water bottles and make our way to the festival ground.

Entering the main grounds, we saw to the right of the main stage a giant Buddha statue with a psychedelic canopy above it and trippy patterns projected onto it.

Next to the main stage were two bars, and to the left of the bars were the market and the food stands. Then even further left was the arts tent, and way in the back were the Mushroom stage; the porta-potties; and the safe zone. We each got a beer and made our way to the Mushroom stage where we spent maybe half an hour, a very short time. We then decided to go to the main stage where we spent the rest of the night on and off.

Unlike my friends, I was born and raised in Canada. I was raised in Toronto for thirteen years and in the countryside an hour north for another thirteen years. Before making aliyah I'd never been to a party, rave, techno, all of the above, never had friends or anything like this. So this was all a first for me. Because of this I was not able to match the energy of my Israeli friends. I told my cousin and friends that while they danced, I was going to walk around with my camera because I wanted to make new friends and meet people. Plus, I'm at my first festival. I need photos.

I started walking around, meeting people on and off. Eventually, at about 5:30 or so, I got a text from Ellie saying that some of our friends went back to camp to take acid. I let her know we'd head back together and I'd meet her at the main stage.

I made my way toward her and started to look for her, hopping on a FaceTime video to show her objects around me as we try to find one another. I eventually find her. But it's not because I spotted her or she spotted me. I only found her because at 6:30 the rockets began. The music eventually

32

stopped, the crowd split up slowly but steadily, and I found my friend Ellie. Grabbing her by the shoulders, I guided us to our friends through the chaos.

When the rockets began people started to leave right away, but many people took their time.

For Israelis this is not totally abnormal: rockets are part of life here. Not being raised here, I had not yet become desensitized to the rockets, but I began looking around and seeing people hurrying to pack up and other people laughing and joking with their friends, smoking or drinking still, poking fun at Hamas, many people thought along the lines of, "Oh the rockets will stop and the party will continue," or "Oh we'll wait for the traffic to calm down and then leave."

We started to discuss if we should leave or stay, deciding how we should go about leaving. There was no arguing, nobody being the boss. Just reasonable back and forth discussion, my friend Yael reading the Red Alert on her phone. Rockets in Netivot, Sderot, Herziliya, Tel-Aviv, Ramat Gan, Ashdod, Ashkelon, etc.

Eventually we decided we'd leave and we started packing up our stuff. I told my cousin, "While you guys pack up, I'm going to go walk around and see if anybody needs a hand with their stuff, and I'm going to take photos." I looked around and still saw people smiling and laughing and joking around with their friends amidst the chaos. So I set out with my camera for thirty to forty minutes doing my thing before I decided to head back. On my way back, faintly off in the distance, I heard gunfire. It was fast and short-lived but I heard it twice. I told this to my cousin and expressed my concern to my friends. Many people were uncertain, but thankfully our stuff was packed and

33

we were ready to go. We said goodbye to the people around us as we left, not realizing it would be the last time anyone would see them alive . . .

We made our way to the car in the parking lot, which was very close to our camp, less than fifty meters away. We began to load the car and were taking our time talking to our friends, Almog, Barak, and Dor by their vehicle. The rockets did not stop. I told my cousin I would go with them because I felt more comfortable with it.

We were deciding who would drive and we settled on me. Most of my friends were on acid. Dor, Ellie, and I were not. I told my cousin that since I'm the most sober, I'll drive. (I also think my cousin drives like a terrorist.) No problem, we all agreed I would drive. Loading our stuff in our car, it was now past 7:30, and I heard gunfire again. But this time, I was not the only one. We all heard it and I think we all sensed something was up. Mordecai, Ellie, Yael, Tamara, and I were in the car, my cousin and I in the front seats. I flew down the dirt path towards the exit, honking my horn and swerving to avoid causing an accident.

Making our way down to the exit amidst the chaos I spotted dozens and dozens of cars blocking one another as they all tried to flee the area down the one road that took us here.

I saw this big wall of traffic stuck in a gridlock and told my cousin, "Fuck that, I don't know them, they're not my friends, they're not my responsibility." I was thinking to myself that I needed to decide fast and not dwell because something was up and I didn't think it was just rockets. Without asking permission, without thinking about damaging his mom's car, I drove off road onto the rocky terrain, afraid I'd get us stuck the whole time, but eventually I made my way to the exit.

I was so close I could see the main road and the police and security guiding people. But I looked around at the other people and cars and I noticed two things: Some cars were empty; others were empty and shut off.

I looked at the car ahead of us. People inside were panicking, honking, and inching forward like you do in traffic when the guy in front doesn't move. I looked at the car ahead of them through their windshield and I saw two things: It was turned off and it was abandoned. I told my cousin, I said, "Mordecai, that car is dead. It's empty. It's not moving, these people are so high and panicked they don't realize it. Please get out and tell them to move because otherwise we're stuck, but they can leave." So my cousin, because he is fluent in Hebrew, tells them what's up and then they drive off and leave. Now it's our turn.

I followed suit and soon was facing the main road where one or two police cars and a mix of security from the festival were directing people. Some instructed people to drive into the fields; others said to drive down the road. But no one was allowed past them, for reasons nobody could have imagined.

I approached, looked left, looked right.

Police said not to go left so I didn't. I didn't realize it was because in that direction, towards Kibbutz Be'eri and Kfar Azza, Hamas was present, brutally murdering people, burning them alive, raping them, etc. To our right, I saw that there was traffic down the road, not realizing the cause was due to Hamas moving up slowly, shooting anybody they saw, blowing them up or burning them in their cars.

All I saw to my right was traffic that I didn't want to deal with, and to my left police telling me to turn the other way, so we listened. I figured I would drive into the field, and maybe we'd find a road or a house. Worst case, we could hide in the woods.

I drove into the field. Other people already had the same idea before us and were already there looking for a way out.

But before we made it thirty meters in, my cousin's girlfriend Tamara suddenly screamed at us to get out of the car and run. We were being shot at. We heard the gunfire ringing out and people were fleeing on foot in every direction or laying down and crouching to avoid being shot.

We all fled the car on foot. My friend Ellie and I were in front, ducking down low to avoid being shot.

Holding onto my friend Ellie so tight I thought I might hurt her, with my back to the festival, I looked around and spotted Tamara and Yael behind us, cowering down low, holding one another to avoid gunfire.

I looked for my cousin and saw the back of his head as he ran back to the car, got in, and came back to pick us up. I no longer cared that he was on acid. I just wanted to be out of there. I pulled my camera off my neck and started photographing again, along with my iPhone, thinking that in case we die, at least there would be proof of everything unfolding.

We drove around aimlessly, looking for escape. People fled on foot into the woods, down the cliff face, or stood on their cars looking for escape routes. Trucks overflowing with people— some hanging off the side—drove through the fields. Eventually, I pointed out a space in an adjacent field and suggested it might be a road. My cousin drove towards it, and we saw that it was in fact a road and a way out. Other people were already there.

As we drove through the orange trees, passing each row, I couldn't help but wonder if there were gunmen hiding there . . .

As we were driving, I learned where Gaza was. Going to my first music festival and arriving at 2:00 a.m., "Where is Gaza?" isn't something you ask. I asked my cousin, "What's the nearest border they'd be coming from?"

He responded with a question, asking me, "What direction is east?"

"Straight ahead, towards the sun because sun rises from the east, why?"

"Because west is Gaza," he answered. That's when I learned how close we were, and when I first thought, "Hamas."

That orange field was probably one minute of driving for us. Every other field was beige and barren. We, along with some other cars, eventually made it to a back road in between these farms and began to follow it. One of the two cars in front of us pulled off to hide behind a warehouse of sorts. We passed some men on bicycles and two Thai workers on motorbikes. Each time we invited them into our car, but they ignored us.

Eventually we and the car ahead of us made it to a real road and we both turned right. Then, for whatever reason, the car ahead of us turned around and waved for us to do the same. My cousin began to but stopped. I think both of us at that point realized they just decided to go back the way of the festival so we kept going in our initial direction. As we drove down this forested road, other cars passed us going the opposite way. My cousin tried to warn them, honking and waving his arm out the window. We hit a few checkpoints. "Are you Israeli? Where are you going?" There followed lots of conversation in Hebrew, but they always asked us, "Are you Israeli? Where are you going?" Our answer was always the same: "Yes. Tel-Aviv."

Rockets were overhead. As we passed the city of Netivot, there were more rockets. We were next to the city now and it was past 8 a.m. The sirens turned on as rockets flew above. Vehicles were all over, a mix of those deliberately parked and those abandoned. We saw IDF border patrol in the intersection and figured it was a checkpoint like the others, put up in response to the incursion by Hamas. But nobody was looking at us, speaking to us, or anything. I suggested that my cousin drive over the median and pass everybody, thinking to myself, "If it's a checkpoint, they'll stop us." But we drove by unhindered. Then we saw ambulance workers around a body on the ground and people hiding in a bunker, and a police car riddled with bullets. We did everything we could to reach Tel-Aviv, avoiding danger and staying as east as possible. We saw abandoned vehicles and bodies everywhere, and IDF checkpoints. Then more and more bodies. I tried to keep filming as much as I could with my hands shaking violently. Bodies were all over the road left and right, in cars or strewn around them. I told my cousin he was a hero, he was saving us, doing such a great job. I tried to keep myself calm and navigate for my cousin, along with his girlfriend. We were on the highway now, driving along, when we saw two men.

As we approached, we saw them and the car beside them very clearly because we were parallel to them.

They were wearing blue jeans, cargo pants, black t-shirts, and black masks, holding rifles. One man had hands red with blood. I could see in the car next to them a man and a woman dead in the front seats. We all screamed at my cousin to drive on, not to stop, and we left as one man raised his gun at us, but nothing more. Passing them, we drove around three more bodies on the road as we continued to flee. We made it back to Tel-Aviv at 9:45 a.m.

But our friends Barak, Almog, and Dor were missing. We heard nothing all day and most of the night until we finally learned they had survived. My next concern was that everyone I made friends with at the festival was dead. At my cousin's apartment, everybody, all of our friends and various relatives, came to be with us. Tel-Aviv was at a standstill, like a ghost town. I waited till Monday to go to the shop to develop my film of the photos at the festival. Running from Neve Sha'anan to Allenby Street, with sirens and rockets overhead the whole time, I got my film developed and scanned, and uploaded the images to Facebook. Throughout October, November, and December, I began learning people's fates. Thankfully nearly everybody survived, but two did not. Dor Avitan and Ran Shaffer, whom I had the pleasure to meet and learn about at the Nova Festival, had died. Learning of their fate, I printed their photos and gave them to their families. Then immediately, on October 9, I begin doing interviews, nearly every day for the whole month. Sometimes six times a day with exclusively western media because I wanted to help, and only know English.

I am now in North America, having traveled here numerous times since October 7, to visit communities all over and schools to share my photos with people and share the magnitude of the situation and let people know what it was like for me.

~

Tohar Hava Pappenheim
Trance

A man is running in the forest, and his disabled daughter is hanging on his arms.

A man is running amok in the forest and his daughter, disabled, is hanging on his shoulders. She suffers from severe muscular dystrophy and cannot run on her own, or even stand without immediately falling to the ground.

The Hamas Nazis with the green ribbons on their guns and on their foreheads shoot everywhere; they scream rage and hatred and thirst for blood. Monsters that the devil pales next to.

When they start shooting at his car, he makes a quick decision to run away, but not before he quickly pulls his Ruth out of the car, puts her arms around his shoulders, and reassures her: "Don't worry, my love, nothing bad will happen to you. Your dad is with you and will never leave you." The beating of the heart, the trembling of the hands, the sweat of the body, the thorns, the stones and the thistles.

And the arms hurt and the running becomes slow, the weight plays against them. If he were alone he might have been able to escape, he might have had a chance, but when she's in his hands this chance is lost.

They are determined and they shoot, aiming to hit, each shot paralyzing him and her with fear. The sight of her crooked limbs leaves no doubt that she is disabled, but they don't care. They want to murder, finish, eliminate.

"Ruth, Daddy won't leave you, do you hear? Dad is with you forever," he shouts to her. He turns his head to her while the bullets threaten to tear their bodies apart. He breathes heavily, his running becomes slow. She growls at him like a wounded animal, screams without words, screams that saw through the air.

"I love you, my Ruth, my whole world," he shouts when he is shot and falls to the ground, and her with him, lying on the ground and the autumn leaves, her aching body, which since her birth has caused her pain and suffering. Her pain ends with one shot. Both are thrown to the ground. They bleed until their hearts stop.

When she was a child, there were people who were insensitive, calling her "crippled," but she and her father, Arik, knew that everyone who had a body was actually limited; the body is a buffer between the person and his soul and his spirituality.

That's why she loved music so much. The music was able to seep into her body and uplift her soul. Music reminded her that there are experiences that penetrate the skin, the blood vessels, the flesh, that touch deeply the innermost essence of a person.

And he took her to all the most prestigious music festivals in Israel and the world, decorated her wheelchair with special lights, dressed her in colorful clothes, danced happily as she turned her wheelchair in circles to the songs she loved so much, ecstatically trying to merge her mind with her body. Eyebrows were raised and questions were asked, but everyone knew and admired this father who was willing to limit his movement and his freedom in order to fulfill the dreams of his daughter who needed constant help with the simplest actions.

And he—whom she knew best, and whose desires and duties were to make her so happy that each morning he thought of her before he thought of himself—went to her bed and kissed her, helped her get from lying down to sitting, moved her to the special bathing chair, took her to the bathroom, held her toothbrush, brushed her teeth, and helped her wash her face.

And when she looked in the mirror at both of them, he smiled at her, and she felt a sense of security and tremendous warmth, the feeling of a person wrapped and protected, an equal, worthy, meaningful person.

Her father did not leave her for a moment, neither in his life nor in his death, because without her he would have no life, and the other way around: especially the other way around.

This post is in their memory.

Arik (Aryeh) and Ruth Peretz, HY"D, may their souls be bound for eternal life—for a quick union in death, in the world of souls, where the limitations of the body do not exist, and the soul is eternal.

There is no end.

~

Sigal Tzur
Everyone's Little Prince

30 days in his memory | My Adi
The blue in the air will fade after this.
What was, will not be again after this.
Nothing will cover the hole in my chest after this.
Giora Fisher, a bereaved father, on his son

My dear child, my sweetheart,

It is with a heavy heart that I sit down to write to you, the seventh of November, exactly one month to the morning of that cursed Saturday when you left still sleepy and in good faith for another shift on that deciding morning of your life, not to return.

It has been a month of the shaking of the soul, a month which begins with your morning message—which will always be the last in the family group—and continues into days of uncertainty, of heavy concerns that increase moment by moment and weigh on each breath. On that cursed Saturday, we gathered ourselves detail by detail, feeling the fear creeping in and overwhelming; clinging to every sliver of a statement and again landing on the harsh facts, which left no room for hope. And then it came, a knock on the door that destroyed our souls and our home—that it's over, that you won't come back. That the life we had will no longer be the same. You fought the last battle of our lives—of your life and my life, which have always been combined together. You made your way out for the last time of the home you loved so much, through the stations of your life, and said goodbye to them. But this time you are

43

accompanied by hundreds of people on the side of the road and thousands who were at your funeral. I am imagining you, surprised, with your small embarrassed and humble smile.

These are the days of Shiva, a painful and intense month in which we've met thousands of people who have visited our home. Some we know and some we don't, but all have wanted to support and comfort us. We have gotten to know many organizations for bereaved families that we instantly became part of, as well as representatives of the Ministry of Defense, who we had previously only heard of, and who now were with us inside our home and becoming part of our lives.

A month that we spent trying to understand your last moments. Trying to figure out the fateful decision that sealed your life. Tracing, learning the details from your friends in the jeep and your commanders, and afterward collecting the findings and answers that were there in the field. You fought there with strength, until the last bullet. The heroism of you and Michael—two snipers in those moments—brought down many terrorists. Your brave and heroic decision, which diverted the heavy fire toward you and allowed the jeep to retreat to the outpost, was the fight of your life that saved your friends and prevented the massacre of the residents of Kissufim. I don't know if you know, Mom's boy, that you died a hero.

The feelings are mixed and range between wincing and astonishment, and they only got stronger when I stood lost in front of your equipment that returned, this time, without you. Your phone, which you'd been waiting so long to replace, arrived smashed to pieces—proof of the immensity of the inferno you were standing in. I feel my heart crashing with those pieces.

This month was a month in which all the media channels found out about you and this preliminary battle, and under your picture was written: "fought bravely." The heroic battle behind Kissufim . . .

We meet your unit mates, hear about the little prince that you were; turns out it wasn't just around us.

You were everyone's little prince. We hear about the inner strength, the inclusion, doing everything for everyone in the battalion as the last samurai. And we hear about your friendship, your good friendship that gave each of them the feeling that they were your best friend. I've thought about how much this says about you. What broke me the most was the post made by the Chaim Shel Acherim nonprofit, from where we adopted your Lenny, about the life you gave her after many years without a home, about the little prince you were for her and the bond and unconditional love between you two. What about her, you must be asking? She feels, my child, she is sad, quiet and waiting for you in your room.

A month of long nights, our minds repeating over and over again your last times with us and how many unknowing goodbyes there were from everyone . . . Starting with the emotional family trip to Ein Gev, our second home, and this time with your Inbalul's family for her twentieth birthday. In retrospect, you said goodbye to the Kinneret (Sea of Galilee), a place deep in your soul. The dinner you made for your friends after Yom Kippur, the challahs you baked for Aunt Idit on Sukkot Eve for a meal with the extended family, and those long days between Kippur and Sukkot, when you were at home as if to say goodbye to everything, to everyone. Even to Lenny . . . I am melting and painfully remembering the minutes before I drove you on your way back to base, when you suddenly dropped your bag and called her for a walk—a final walk—almost like you felt you had to say goodbye to all your loved ones.

The abysmal sadness in Inbal's young eyes—your Balul mourns the loss of the love of her life and what the future was supposed to bring—it tears me apart, wounds and hurts me. Inbal, who grew up quickly, is hurt but continues to do things in your honor . . . Unfathomable, unbearable!

It is impossible to describe the relationship we had even with words. You always trusted me, that I would fix everything . . . that I would not give up, that I would move mountains if necessary, and so you wrote in my birthday card, November 2022:

> My Mamo, it's true that a lot of times life gives us unexpected things to work with, but once you know how to work with them, there's no doubt that people become stronger. Every time something unexpected happens, you rise above all expectations and show us all why we admire you so much. The way you work, the way you always excel, is something that not everyone can do and it's something that I have to learn from you. Sometimes you can just be called Superman, because I really feel that you can do anything . . .

So honestly, no, my son, I am not all-powerful . . . As the days pass, the feeling of sorrow and the knowledge of this unbearable reality fills every part and pore of my body. I feel how my inner strength is being emptied, and the hole in my heart and soul is huge. For the first time in my life, my child, your optimistic, all-powerful mother feels so lost. Defeated. Broken. Lacking. Emptied. Tormented. And I miss you so much.

I love you so much, you are forever in my heart, in the depths of my soul and in my breaths until the end. Your Mamo.

+ + +

What blessings can I give this child,
what can he be blessed with?
Asked the angel
And he blessed him with a smile, bright as light
And he blessed him with big observing eyes
With them to catch every flower,
Every living creature or bird
And with a heart to feel what he sees.
What blessings can I give this youth?
What can he be blessed with?
Asked the angel
And he blessed him with legs to dance forever
And a soul to remember all tunes
And a hand to collect shells on the beach
And an ear attentive to old and young
What blessings can I give this young man?
What can he be blessed with?
Asked the angel
And he blessed that his hands which are used to flowers
Will succeed in learning the might of the steel
And his legs to dance the road's journey
And lips to sing the command pace
What blessings can I give this man?
What can he be blessed with?
Asked the angel
I gave him all I could give

A song a smile and legs to dance
And a delicate hand and a trembling heart
What else can I bless you with?
This boy is now an angel
No one will bless him, he will never be blessed
God God God If only you blessed him with life.

~

Hodaya Harush
Live Alongside It and Not Inside It

My husband, my Eli

How can I talk about you in the past tense?

You are the most beautiful flower in the garden that was picked before your time

The entire Black Shabbat I had hope that you would walk through the door

Smile your smile and tell me—you think anyone would dare to mess with me?!

But here you fought bravely and courageously I'm sure you were the first to respond and engage

You are brave like no other

You were in the direct line of the wrongdoers and protected your teammates with your body

You gave your soul for kiddush Hashem ("sanctification of God" in Judaism)

Kiddush Hashem that will not bring you back to me

You have a place in heaven to which you have ascended immediately

How did you leave me a widow and your daughters orphans Lia, Ofri and Noya

And your parents and siblings bereaved

How am I going to celebrate Ofri's birthday this Thursday without her dad?!?!???!

You would enter the house after a tiring shift, the girls would run and not leave you, your face would immediately light up for them, you'd hug them, kiss them and bring them something sweet to make them happy

You would go out to smoke a cigarette and they would fight to get out with you to earn more time with you another minute another second as if they felt and knew things that I didn't

You would take care of me and them pampering helping caring and accommodating

You are truly a loss to an entire nation

To me, as a husband

A father to the girls

A son and brother to your parents and siblings

A member of the unit who always made sure personally as a shift manager to be the first to take care of them and help

Every place I went I heard compliments about you

How humble, how modest you are and how you do your work faithfully

If only you could come back to me again I would tell you

My kinggggg, my love

Unconditional love I love you to the sky but there is no return because you stayed there forever

HY"D, you were and remain a hero and brave

You will always be in my heart forever

Pray for us and be an advocate of honesty to all the people of Israel. I love you. I ask you for forgiveness. Forgive me, my dear husband.

~

Yadid Didi Shohat
Beginning of the War—
Medical Teams on the Frontline

Saturday, October 7, 2023

06:34—Alarm in the village. My wife, Raz, wakes me; we gather the children and enter the safe room.

A crazy sequence of alarms, it seems strange.

Raz tells me, "Strange—since we moved to the village about three years ago, we haven't had such a large number of back-to-back alarms."

The children in the safe room have already lost sleep, a steady sequence of alarms. We are taking one child at a time to use the bathroom. Later Raz goes out to brush her teeth and then I go.

While I'm brushing my teeth, Raz hears a strange noise outside and asks, "What is this noise?"

I stop brushing and hear nothing.

I finish brushing, say morning blessings, and prepare something warm for the kids to drink—so they can at least pass the time in the safe room. I'm optimistic, approach the closet, take the Psalms book, thinking it's better that I start reading Psalms until the alarms stop, and then I'll go to the synagogue.

07:22—The phone rings; it feels odd because on Saturdays, the phone doesn't just ring randomly. Only residents of the village call on Saturdays, in case of a medical event or the MDA (emergency medical services) center updating me on a medical event in the village.

I answer the call; Liz is on the line: "We have an ambulance driver shot in the area of Urim Junction. Can you go replace him?"

Of course, I tell her, starting to get dressed, at the same time calling my brother Hagai and asking him and his wife to come to us and stay with Raz and the kids. Meanwhile, a continuous sequence of alarms in the village that doesn't stop.

07:26—I'm already ready, waiting for my brother Hagai, while the alarms ring continuously in the village. Hagai arrives, I leave the house, and Raz is confident that within an hour I'll be back home; that's usually what happens when I leave home to provide medical assistance.

I open the car, hear the alarm again, approach a concrete wall, and lie down on the floor. The alarm stops, I hear a bunch of gunshots, and then I understand that this was the noise Raz heard when I was brushing my teeth. I get up, run to the car, and again an alarm sounds, again I'm on the floor. The alarm stops, I get into the car, take the gun from the holster and place it between my legs, and speed to Urim Junction, calling Peter on the way. He's the intensive care ambulance driver—maybe he'll answer me—but there's no response. I arrive at Urim Junction, look for the yellow MDA treatment ambulance, see many cars and people, but can't find the ambulance.

Up to the present day, I have been pondering what I saw there and I can't remember. It was like tunnel vision.

I call Danny, and he tells me that he is currently driving in the intensive care ambulance, and they are on their way to the Gilat Junction to meet up with a team from Beit She'an.

I leave the Urim Junction toward the Gilat Junction, speeding along the road, or rather flying low. I have never seen this speed on the speedometer before. Arriving at the Merhavim square, the car barely stops, almost going up onto the square. I keep flying low, not sure what color the traffic lights are on the way, but I pass all of them without stopping, I reach the Gilat Junction, and they have already moved Peter to the second intensive care ambulance.

Danny is returning to the intensive care ambulance and asks me to follow him to the station in Ofakim.

Arriving at the MDA station in Ofakim, I see that volunteers and workers have already taken all the ambulances and gotten reinforcements from additional teams.

At the station we are organizing protective equipment under pressure, amidst alarms in the city and its surroundings. Rumors about the situation in the sector and the city are already circulating.

Danny and Yan arrive with an emergency ambulance after a night shift in Ramat Hovav. Suddenly a small private car enters the station at high speed with two injured people inside. One of them is already unconscious. We begin treating him, he loses his pulse, we start administering CPR, and realize that unfortunately we are unable to help him; they place him aside.

We move on to the second injured man. He still has a vest and a gun; we start removing them and the clothes. A mobile phone falls, and the screen lights up with an Arabic inscription on it. Everyone takes a step back for a second and then sees a wallet—there is a police ID inside. We return to the mission, treatment, preparation for evacuation, Danny and Yan on the way with him to Soroka.

Another vehicle arrives, four with gunshot wounds, soldiers and civilians. We put them in the regular ambulance; I'm with them in the back. Linoy gets in and starts driving, and we start leaving the station. Danny stops us: "There's another wounded man, policeman—take him with you." The policeman has a gunshot wound in the leg; he sits next to Linoy the driver. The window is open, weapon drawn; he secures us during the trip.

I ask Linoy to go out through the main entrance of the city and bring us to Soroka Medical Center as quickly as possible. She does it very quickly; it feels like an eternity to me.

Crazy ride, five with gunshot wounds in the ambulance— never happened to me. On the way I perform quick tests, stop bleeding, and replace arterial blockage, trying to calm the wounded, maybe myself too.

We arrive at Soroka Hospital, where everyone is already prepared. They help us unload the wounded. We organize quickly and return to the MDA Ofakim station.

The picture is not clear yet, but the teams already understand that this is a war for our home.

All day long we spend between the alarms and the sounds of gunfire, treating the injured, taking shelter, trying to keep in touch with our families and still stay focused.

I receive a message from Raz, a picture of the house. I open it; the house is full of people.

There are tons of people here who ran away from a party, she writes to me.

You are my life, my heart
You are a righteous one
I answer her and go back to organizing things.

Again a message from Raz, a voice message. She still doesn't know what's going on, exactly, and is asking me to come back home.

I write her a message.

We are all here at the station

Everything is fine

This is a war for our home

I receive a phone call. "Hey, Yadid, I heard you live in Patish Village. Someone who was with you in the army gave me your phone number. My brother was at a party in Re'im; I understood from him that they are on their way to Petish. Can I let him into your house?"

I gladly tell her, "I'm not at home, I'm at the MDA. Send me his number, I'll do everything I can."

I finish the conversation with her, call him, try to point him in the direction of the village, send him a location for navigation on the map, and go out to the event.

While treating and evacuating casualties I receive more calls and messages, ask them to call, treat the injured in the ambulance, and try to help the families by phone. After several phone calls I give up and give them the number of Raz and Hagai. They are in the village now, and they will be able to help them more than I can.

Crazy day, conversations with my family, everyone is stressed. Video calls with my son Ariel are heartbreaking; he has tears in his eyes; he is angry with me for not coming back yet. In the morning he asked Hagai why they aren't going to the synagogue.

While evacuating and treating injured people we are informed of the opening of a casualty treatment point and a slain-soldiers point at the MDA Ofakim station; this indicates the number of injured. My brother Hagai is calling me; he also caught the MDA bug. He recently finished a course for volunteer medics at the MDA, and he arrived at the community center in the village to take care of the wounded and survivors of the party that took place in Re'im along with residents of the village, medical personnel, and non-medical personnel.

Hagai calls. "We have gunshot and shrapnel wounded here, some have been bandaged, some have received an arterial tourniquet, and there are some who came to us at the village with arterial tourniquets on them. Is it possible to send a vehicle to evacuate them?"

"I don't think so," I answer. "There is a large number of casualties, so we opened a treatment point at the station. Evacuate them to us if you can."

During the day there are rumors about little Aharon. He left the house with an ambulance to treat gunshot wounds, and since then he has not answered the phone or the walkie talkie. Unfortunately, a few hours later we learn that he was murdered by the damned terrorists while he was going to save innocent Israelis.

During one of the evacuations to Soroka Hospital I meet Dekker, a very dear man, an entertainer, optimistic and a smiler. I have known him since I was a child. Dekker is already in his army uniform, was recruited into the reserves in the Home Front Command. He tells me that he came to Soroka Hospital with the district commander who was wounded in a shootout with the terrorists at the Urim base. With an odd coolness he tells me that his son Naor, who is serving in Golani, has lost contact. "We don't know what's going on with him," he tells me in a cold way that I still can't understand. To our great regret, a few days later we are informed that this hero was killed in battle against the damned terrorists.

A hard day, physical and mental fatigue, fighting for our home, treating a lot of injured people, traveling all over the region. Lying to Raz, my dear wife, and my dear mother, I promise in every message and in every call that I will only stay at the station and not go anywhere.

During the day, more and more details about the situation are revealed. In retrospect it turns out that leaving the Urim Junction in the morning meant a journey into hell: the terrorists passed through there, massacred everyone who crossed their path. Some continued to Ofakim and some to the Home Front Command base in Urim, where the beloved Ofir, my children's babysitter, was killed in a shootout.

I pass by there, I look for the intensive care ambulance. It's yellow, big, and prominent. That's the only thing I still remember seeing.

Slowly the picture becomes clearer; we hear about more and more missing and dead people who, along with their families, are part of our lives.

Thank you very much to the Holy One, blessed be He, for His protection
May we know better days with God's help
May we see all the captives and abductees return to us safe and sound with God's help, in memory of friends and acquaintances
The late Ofir Davidian
The late Naor Siboni
The late Aviv Hajaj
The late Aharon Haimov

The late Avia (Aboya) Hezroni
The late Amit Man
The late Yarin Peled
And all the citizens, policemen, soldiers and security and
rescue personnel who were murdered on this damned day
May God resurrect your blood

~

Shavit Berglas
Two Weeks and a Day Later

Today is two weeks and a day later . . .
Thinking of those moments.

October 7, 23, 6:31 a.m., Sabbath

We wake up to massive Red Alert sirens. Uri, my partner, receives a message about a shooting victim, terror attack. Several shots are heard in the kibbutz. Uri dresses, takes his personal weapon, and tells me to get dressed quickly. We begin to wonder how we can bring our Mika from her apartment, tens of meters away from us, here to us. Meanwhile, Uri receives a telephone call for help. He leaves in that direction and finds himself in a shooting match with a group of terrorists. He meets Doron, a soldier, the son of a kibbutz member. They take cover and agree that Doron will fetch his weapon and join Uri. Together they rescue Mika under fire and bring her to the safe room in our house. Uri and Doron position themselves in the pergola on the second floor. The pergola is covered with branches from a big tree. It faces the main road of the kibbutz. They are both armed. A group of terrorists approaches; Uri and Doron kill them.

More terrorists arrive. Another battle. And so on. The minutes/hours pass, and another group of terrorists arrives with a pickup truck to take us. Bravely and with no helmets or safety vests, when another shooting battle starts, Uri and Doron manage to kill them too, puncturing the wheels of the truck, which disables the vehicle and blocks the way for other vehicles. Time passes and no help comes.

They are all alone on the pergola. All around they hear

shooting and shouts in Arabic. Mika and I are in the safe room listening to the bullets exploding on the metal window, on the ceiling, and all around the safe room. Moments of silence between the battles, and I am sure that the worst has happened. Seconds feel like hours. And then a sign from Uri. I breathe again.

Later, Uri tells us that during the battles, Doron's ammunition ran out. They descended from the pergola while covering each other with Doron's last bullet remaining, they took Kalashnikovs and ammunition from the dead terrorists, and they continued fighting from the pergola. Mika and I in the safe room, we play the "city, country" game by the light of a small lamp. She beats me easily.

Most of the time we are in the dark, I hold a bottle of perfume and two metal lamps. If they come, Mika and I will fight. We are in a practical state of mind. No pressure. Determined. At approximately 16:00 hours, Uri and our neighbor, who continued to fight although he had been injured, decide to join forces and take us together with some soldiers who arrived at our neighbor's safe room, all the while under attack. Coming out we see seven dead terrorists thanks to Doron and Uri, and also the punctured pickup with a dead terrorist still at the wheel. Those were the terrorists who came to kill us or kidnap us, as well as everyone in all the surrounding apartments. In the neighbor's safe room are his wife, his five children, and their brave dog, Chips.

Mika reads stories to the children. We chat on WhatsApp with Itzik Ozeri, the clown; the children are happy to hear his voice in the message he's sent. All the while, we are continuing to receive all the terrifying messages our friends are sending, which tell us that the terrorists have entered their homes, that they are being taken, they are being shot at, their houses are being burnt, and they are choking. At about 18:00 hours, it is finally decided that we will leave the safe room. They remove us very carefully. A line of soldiers on the right, another on the left, and we run with the children on our backs. On the way we see sights which I will not write about. Red Alert sirens begin, and we hear a loud boom. At the gathering space, at the entrance to the kibbutz, Mika and I wait to be evacuated by bus. We see many injured along the way . . . we get on the bus and drive toward the center. Uri remains at the gathering space. There, he assists in tending to the injured who arrive. Yes. Uri is a fighter and a medic. Along the way are sights I will not describe. We arrive in Tel Aviv, and our Aloni is waiting for us with a big embrace full of love and concern. I recharge my phone and speak with our Shovali. I try to calm her; she is convinced she is going to lose her family. And only because her father is a brave fighter, who by chance met a very brave young soldier, were we saved.

After three days we begin to understand the extent of the devastation.

Today, two weeks later, the devastation is still being revealed. The tragedy is ongoing. Every day we get word of the death of another victim who was out of communication, and every day there are funerals.

So many of our friends, girls and boys, babies and entire families, were murdered.

And all of them, I knew all of them. Many of them I knew personally—we worked together, we ate together, we trained together, we lived together in a beautiful kibbutz that has been destroyed by insane, cruel murderers.

~

61

Tamar Habilio
Our Sun

Hey, my friend, I'm writing you because I don't know what else to do; you're the only person I want to talk to right now. It's been a month since you've gone and it feels like two decades. You'd already been in South America for a year, and although I missed you and talked about you every day, I survived it. And somehow every day in the last month was like that year you were in South America, only in South America you would answer my FaceTime calls and called me when you had time, and when I didn't answer you would write me a hundred separate messages that I'm trash for ignoring you. You haven't called me trash for a month, and that's what I miss the most in the world.

On Saturday I was at the beach. The last time I was at the beach, we were together, remember? You convinced me that it was a beautiful day and it would be fun, and you came with your huge cup of cold coffee and your beach bag full of everything, and we went to your secret corner that you loved and of course I didn't know. So on Saturday when I went to the beach, you didn't have to convince me like you always did. I immediately wanted to go, because I knew you would be there, because it was Saturday, and your favorite thing to do on the weekend is to be with friends and be at the beach. So on Saturday the beach was empty and the water was crystal clear—all in all, I don't need to tell you because you were there with me. I played backgammon with Kelly and I won; remember no one wanted to teach me because everyone thought I would be bad, and only you agreed? I have no doubt that you arranged the dice when I played so that I would win, because if it's not against you, you don't mind congratulating me on my victory. You should also know that I found the most beautiful seashells in the sea. It's clear to me that you arranged them in places that you knew I would look, so that I would find them.

So somehow a month has passed, and every day is worse because I'm afraid I'll start to forget—how your smile is big and bright, and how your golden hair shines, and how every word you say is like a warm hug. I wanted to say thank you for reminding me that if I'm afraid or start to forget about the sun that you are, I can go to the sea and meet you there, in the warm sand, in the golden sun, in the clear water on the smooth shells in the noisy silence of the waves, because it's you, and you will be there waiting to hug me when it's hard for me and when it's too heavy for me, like you've always been.

~

Yuval Zeituny
My Rotem: Smiles, Purity, and a Moon That Will Shine for Eternity

I was supposed to eulogize Rotem, but how can I eulogize Totem . . .

There are friends, and then there is Dy Totem.

That is the nickname I gave you from the first moment: Dy Totem.

The D, a typo which we had decided was good enough to keep.

There are friends, and then there is Dy Totem.

We meet people during our lives, and as we both believed, there are those who stay for a while and those who are forever.

We concluded that there is no friendship like ours as we are first sisters and then friends.

A few weeks back when I was going through a tough time and of course, as always, you were there for me, you asked five times in one day where I was, and I said that I was at work until 16:00 hours, as usual.

I asked you why you asked me so often, and you replied that you wanted to bring me something. My first thought was that you wanted to bring me flowers, as that was our thing, flowers.

You arrived wearing a little black dress covering your beautiful thin body, delicate and pure, and you gifted me a notebook with my name printed on the cover that you had bought, with a sticker you had prepared and a dedication you'd written, and you told me that recently you had begun writing all your thoughts in a notebook, and that now it was my turn to get a notebook.

Typical of me, I started crying in the middle of work, in front of clients, and thanked you for thinking of me.

You said to me, sister, be quiet, what is wrong with you?

Rotem Neiman, you are everyone's best friend, you give everyone their perfect place in your life, and it amazes me how I always say that I don't have time, but somehow you magically have space for all your friends in such a wonderful way; you are everyone's best friend.

You appeared like a beautifully wrapped gift, with sweets and ribbons of pure happiness and laughter, with an irresistible and captivating smile. I can envision your rolling laughter in my head; it is deeply ingrained.

On your birthday we all came to celebrate with you, and the place was packed with people. I asked you, Totem, is there a chance that all these people are your friends? You said no way, it's impossible. Look how many there are. And I said to you, it's crazy, they all love you. How could they not?

I brought you flowers and slipped a letter into your bag, and you wrote me to tell me that you found the letter with the message saying that I will be with you forever. Then you took a photo every second day you had the flowers, and each time we spoke we discussed each flower and its shape and what an amazing creation a flower is.

In my mind I reflect on recent times, on our conversations, and on how fortunate we are to have such a huge, wonderful family from our trip, how lucky we were to find such a united family, and now this family without you is embracing and crying as our sister has been taken from us, the glue and the night flower, the most accessible and beautiful I have ever known, the most inspiring, spreading her pollen all around.

This family promises to stay together as you know it, the closest in the entire world. It will take time, but we will continue to celebrate and to enjoy ourselves just like you loved to do.

~

The Zionist Leadership Fund
Rescue from the Carnage

Ben Binyamin Shimoni, thirty-one years old, from Ashkelon.

Ben Binyamin Shimoni attended the party in Re'im, succeeded in escaping by the skin of his teeth, and managed to get to Be'er Sheva.

Along the way he called his brother Avinoam, who told him to collect their mother from Ashkelon and to come up north to him.

His girlfriend too, who was hiding from the terrorists, begged him not to return to Re'im.

But Ben had other plans. The thought that he had been saved but others—among them his close friend Tom—were still there at the mercy of these animalistic people who were butchering them, torturing, raping, and kidnapping them—did not align with his noble personality, which was so pronounced on that Shabbat.

His brother describes his personality as "always putting himself last and wanting to help."

And so, even though he was unarmed, in Be'er Sheva he dropped off the five partygoers he had rescued, turned the car around, and made his way back to Re'im to save his friend Tom, even though Tom had specifically told him not to return to the area, which was swarming with terrorists.

Ben's reply to Tom: "Send me your coordinates."

Tom, with 2 percent battery power remaining, did not succeed in doing so, and the conversation was disconnected.

Ben raced back to the party site. On arrival, under continuous fire in an area controlled by the terrorists, he opened the doors of the jeep and called to anyone who could to get inside.

And so, at a speed of 170 kmh (Ben, a loved and successful entrepreneur and restauranteur, was also an experienced race-car driver), under continuous fire from the terrorists and rockets falling close by, he rescued another eight partygoers, he threw personal items from his car to make space for more survivors, and he returned to save more people.

The gaps in what actually happened have been filled by twelve partygoers he saved, who contacted the family and his girlfriend after his photograph was revealed and they recognized the angel who saved them.

It is not just the descriptions from the survivors he rescued in his car that are testimony to his calmness, his focus, and his extreme composure.

His telephone locations show that Ben, who understood that the road leading to the party area was blocked by the terrorists, bypassed the road in a huge U-turn and arrived at the scene with his jeep from the rear, from the west, from the area of the compromised border fence.

Ben picked up his last load. His girlfriend, Jessica, was on the line. "I could hear girls he had rescued screaming in the car," she says. "I could hear Ben accelerating, and then silence. The conversation was disconnected."

Ben was wounded and killed, but before he died he managed to save twelve lives.

Thy beauty, O Israel, upon thy high places is slain! How are the mighty fallen!

In his memory.

~

Gadi Wilcherski
I Understand, But . . .

My friends always ask me, "Gadi, seriously, Gadi, why do you go to these parties, why do you travel so far, with a mat and an icebox, in the middle of the night, to the end of the world, turning left and then right, following the signs, like you're looking for the Smurfs' village? Really, what are you trying to find there?"

I try to explain it to them, but a stranger to these parties would not understand: this is our safe space.

From all corners of our nation, the entire human rainbow, gentle people come, who in their daily lives dress up as tough, and at the entrance we allow ourselves to shed the hard shells and to run to the party area to be who we really are.

At the entrance we do a small ritual with ourselves: we make a pact with ourselves to break down all barriers, to release all restraint, to become vulnerable for a few hours. We know, and it is clear to us, that we are in a safe place. Here we will not be judged, here we will be accepted for who we are, here we do not have to make an effort to act like we are fine, here we can also be not okay, here we can finally be ourselves, and damn the world, it is great to be ourselves . . . such a relief, such a joy, such a chorus, such a celebration of love at the core of it all.

And then the worst thing ever happened.

And the worst was really bad. The red was very red. The monsters were monstrosities. The shots sounded sevenfold. RPG rockets flew in front of our eyes, landed, and exploded the bubble of love. People who had come to forget their traumas, or at least to soften them, hoping for some release, suddenly their open and exposed eyes were witness to sights which no human

69

anywhere at any time could bear to see. They were without the most basic defenses a human should have. They were unable to bear even a milligram of violence. I remember how it felt when my heart shrank, seeing someone pushed under a tree, how one winces and is shocked at just the thought of someone far away raising a hand to another. Now take that and multiply it by a million—sensory overload, what a disaster.

Then their souls fled for their souls.

They ran terrified, and around them the world blazed.

It is a nightmare out of hell; it is a nightmare that is endless. Anyhow, when you are exposed like that, you lose all sense of time.

You go home and count the dead, find out who was kidnapped, are exposed to videos. Slowly you begin to understand, slowly you internalize—your tribe has been massacred. You read in the papers what happened at the same time in the nearby villages, and it seems like a bad chapter from the Bible. It seems imaginary, made up, because people do not act with such evil . . . or maybe they do? It is not possible that something this evil could really happen. There are no movies like this, no scripts like this, there just is no such thing. And here we have it—it happened to us. And it hasn't ended yet. No post-trauma, as the trauma is ongoing, and feelings of guilt arise like another monster: Maybe I could have done something more? Maybe I could have saved another person? Why did I survive? Why were all those fairies and angels slaughtered when I am in one piece at home; how can I live with this burden? How will I regain my confidence in the world, in people, in the belief that good will come? How can anything be good! How can we go out on the streets? I am so sad, angry, disappointed, ashamed, hurt, injured, and this hole in my heart that cannot be sealed, the trauma, continues and continues. We are still being attacked, and hundreds have been kidnapped. How am I supposed to get up in the morning and get on with my life?

My loving tribe, I bleed with you. I feel your pain, I am with you, among you, holding your hand. My heart is burning.

~

Adi Kempner
A Three-Year-Old Girl. Alone. In Gaza.

I'm sitting here watching Channel 13.

Watching and crying—my heart is shattering into pieces.

A report on Roee Idan, a *Ynet* photographer who left his home in Kibbutz Kfar Aza to photograph the terrorists who had infiltrated the kibbutz on paragliders.

These monsters came to his house and shot and killed his wife, Smadar, in front of his small children: Michael, age nine, Amalia, age six, and Abigail, age three.

Roee was outside holding Abigail, age three, in his arms. He was also shot, and fell to the ground.

Michael, the hero, a child of just nine years, called the Magen David Adom and told them that his parents were dead, that there were terrorists, and asked for help. The sympathetic telephone receptionist who was with him on the line understood that she had to try to save the children and suggested that they hide.

This hero, a nine-year-old boy, took his sister, Amalia, and together they crept inside a closet in the safe room and hid there from the terrorists for fourteen hours.

Fourteen hours!

Without food, without water, unable to go to the toilet. They sat in total silence until they were rescued.

Roee disappeared and his whereabouts are still unknown; we know he was injured. Three-year-old Abigail has disappeared.

She cannot be found.

A three-year old girl alone.

After seeing what happened to her parents, she's probably
    been kidnapped to Gaza. Alone!
A three-year-old girl in Gaza alone.
A three-year-old girl in Gaza alone.
A three-year-old girl in Gaza alone.
A three-year-old girl in Gaza alone.
Can anyone imagine such a thing?
A three-year-old girl in Gaza alone.
And not one member of this insane government has
    spoken to her family.
I just cannot grasp this . . .
A three-year-old girl in Gaza alone.
Without her father.
Without her mother.
Without her brother.
Without her sister.
With no familiar face.
I cannot stop crying!
My heart is torn.
I cannot grasp this.
Where is the world:
Where are the United Nations?
Where?
A three-year-old girl in Gaza alone!
A little girl, a hero, loved.
I embrace you strongly.
Send you light and good energy.
Embrace you with love.
And pray that still today you will be rescued from this
    hell you are in.

Yoseph Haddad:

Report this to the world, please.

A three-year-old girl alone.

It is impossible to digest.

In addition to my prayers for Abigail, I pray for all the
      other sweet children, our heroes, for all the kid-
      napped, the captives and the missing.

Amen, may they return healthy in body and soul.

Three-year-old Abigail was released after fifty days in Hamas captivity in the Gaza Strip as part of a hostage-prisoner swap between Israel and Hamas in November of 2023 that saw the release of some, not all, of the hostages taken by Hamas. Abigail's parents were murdered on October 7; she returned from captivity an orphan. She now lives with her extended family members.

~

David Panai
Dancing for Release to Serenely Lose Control

I wanted to thank you.
  Thank you for opening my heart that for so many years
      has been sealed.
  Thank you for making me understand that I can love
  and be loved equally.
  I know that since we took these photographs
  we managed to break up and fall in love again.
  But it is still important for me to thank you.
  Because without you my heart would still be sealed.
  You taught me that it is okay to open my heart.
  To decide to be vulnerable, not to hide
  in that secret room which blocks feelings.
  You taught me to take chances, even if
  there is a chance I won't be loved.
  You always believed our meeting was not coincidental.
  Despite the age difference you taught me a lot.
  You filled me with new optimism. Thank you for that!
  I will always remember our deep conversations,
  our laughter and the special way in which you returned
      my love.
  I remember you told me that at age fifteen
  you would go alone to parties.
  I remember how surprised I was, I remember how it
  made me look at you with admiration.
  We always said and agreed that we have commitments
  in life, like taxes and electricity, water.
  But there are the fun things, fun things we need to
      preserve.

Not to neglect, not to forget, to release, to dance
and not to stop until our feet hurt.
We always said that everyone should
lose control serenely. I am happy that you made sure
to do it right, even when we were not together.
I think with you was the first time
in my life that I felt complete in the way I returned your
    love.
All the time we were together I loved you very deeply.
From the day we met until we parted.
I was deeply touched that you were present.
I remember when we met a long time
after we had separated. I remember
that I said I was sorry.
That as I had grown up an orphan from a very young age
I have fear of abandonment, mother issues which I'm
    learning to deal with.
I was sorry that I had been strange some of
the time. I was embarrassed by it. I remember you looked
    at me, placated me, and said everything was alright.
I saw you even when you thought I didn't.
I remember you telling me
"You are all one big heart," and immediately thereafter
you thanked me. Thank you
for changing me from a young girl into a woman.
You always knew to say beautiful words
which made me feel good.
Thank you for that, my Shine Shine.
I came across that terrible video just by chance.
That is not how I want to remember you.

Definitely not! You do not deserve that. I am comforted
    knowing
that you danced and lost control serenely!
As we always said, like you always did.
To be at the height of the party in the lion's share of the
    space.
I feel sad that we live in a world where what we believed
    in is also what caused you not to survive.
I love you, Shani Louk
In my heart there is a portion of real estate which belongs
    only to you.
And will be yours forever.
Thank you.

~

Mary Varon
Amit Man—Your Light Will Shine Forever

Friday morning, October 6, Simchat Torah, I send you a message asking if you can change your shift and come to us together with our mother for the Sabbath, as we miss you terribly and want you to come.

You record a voice message: "If only, Maryum, but I am on call this Sabbath at the Kibbutz. I'll take a rain check on your invitation and come another time."

On that cursed Sabbath of October 7, at six thirty in the morning we wake up to the sound of sirens. At the time you are still at your apartment in the safe room at Kibbutz Be'eri. A friend who is with you invites you to come with him in his car and to drive to Netivot, but you decline and tell him that you are the paramedic on call at the kibbutz, and you have to remain there in case you are needed.

Your friend leaves, and you stay in the safe room in your apartment (the same apartment that later we find out the terrorists did not enter).

In the spur of the moment, you decide to take your medical bag and run while the sirens sound to the dental clinic of the kibbutz. Very quickly you understand that terrorists have infiltrated the kibbutz. You are stuck there at the clinic for seven long, difficult hours, and you slowly begin to understand that you will not be getting out alive. You gather yourself and invest all of yourself in saving the lives of the wounded who manage to get to the clinic. One of the survivors fled from the carnage while shot and wounded, a survivor who tells us afterward that he is alive only thanks to you! He tells us that even when all your medical supplies ran out, you improvised a tourniquet,

78

took care of him, stroked his head, and reassured him with your lovely angelic voice.

All through those long hours, the only thing that interests you is the well-being of those you cannot help. You call Magen David Adom and describe coolly and professionally the wounds of each of the injured and beg for evacuation and assistance for them.

With us, with your family, you allow yourself every now and then to break down a bit. To be afraid . . . and to beg for help, help which we promise will come, any moment now, and rescue you from there.

Saturday noon, the hours pass and no help arrives. The ammunition of the two members of the security squad protecting you at the clinic, who were able to repel the terrorists, is running out and almost fully depleted. The time is 14:00, and you send a message saying that they are entering the clinic and that you will not get out alive. Mom and I call you, and you answer us in tears, screaming that you have been shot in the legggg, Mari, they shot meeee, they are here, they will kill me, help me, Mariiiii, I love you all; Mom, forgive me for everything . . .

And the call is disconnected.

I remain with the telephone at my ear, silent, stunned, frozen in time! I realize that at the other end, vile terrorists are murdering my beautiful little sister, shooting her to death. There is no way to describe the feeling of such helplessness and bewilderment in those dark moments.

What happened to you? Are you dead? Wounded? Kidnapped? Only after two long days—fifty hours, to be exact—comes that dreaded knock at the door, and we are informed that your body has been found.

Everyone who knows us knows what you meant to me, Amitush, my little baby, my enormous pride, my perfect flower. You will always remain all of that to me, and now not only we know the amazing person you were, the entire Israeli nation knows about the brave twenty-two-year-old paramedic, the hero who dedicated her whole life from a young age to saving lives. In the moment of truth, she saved others' lives until her last breath.

Our hearts are broken and splintered, but our spirit is strong and solid.

We pray for the speedy recovery of all the wounded and the return of all the hostages to the arms of their families.

~

Haviva Man
Amit, Our Little Sister, the Greatest of All

Like Sheep to the Slaughter

My amazing sister Amit, only twenty-two years old, a paramedic at Kibbutz Be'eri who saves lives and trains paramedics, waited for seven and a half hours—an eternity!—at the clinic with wounded and dead begging and pleading that they be rescued. Seven and a half hours hiding in the small kitchen with a kitchen knife, listening to the war waging outside, the explosions and the shots! Seven and a half hours during which she, and we, asked: where is the army? Where are the rescuers?

And I promise her that help is on the way, that she will be strong, all will be over soon.

Seven and a half hours!

And then the message from her: "They are here, they are in the clinic, I don't think I will survive, I love you."

And then after some moments that felt like eternity and she did not respond, I gave it another desperate try. I called her. She answered me, screaming that she had been shot in the leg, that they had murdered everyone there, and she was the last one alive—they were on to her! I heard shots and the call disconnected.

As of 14:15, we lost touch with her.

We are praying for a miracle. Hoping she is still alive.

All the progress, the might, the technology, one big zero!

My Amit, my love, give us a sign of life.

81

Update

There is no news of Amit. She was not among the hostages
from the kibbutz. We still do not know where she is and what
has happened to her. No official entity has spoken to us even
once to update us on anything, not even to tell us that they are
trying to find her.

The last time I spoke to her, she was at the clinic in Be'eri.
If anyone in Be'eri knows anything, saw, heard . . .

Please! Any bit of information about her will help. Thank
you all for your support, your prayers, and your embraces.

Amen, Amen, Amen, our Amitush, come back to us.

Update

That's it. It's over. With infinite sorrow and the deepest pain, I
inform you that our amazing, beautiful, brave, intelligent Amitush has been murdered by inhumane terrorists.

May the memory of my little sister be blessed for eternity.

The funeral will take place tomorrow (Tuesday) at 15:30
at the Netivot Cemetery.

We understand that Amit was at the dental clinic at the
kibbutz.

Does anyone know if the clinic has been checked? Does
anyone know the nurse that was there with them? (I don't
know her name).

~

Idit Nevo
Instead of a Wedding—a Funeral

In memory of the Israeli hero Major Jamal Abbas, RIP.

I've been trying for a day to find the right words to describe the funeral of Jamal and how heartbroken I am. I hope my words will succeed in describing some of my feelings and the level of respect and love that I feel for the Abbas family. And if not, forgive me.

In the photographs, some of which I am posting here, we see Jamal, the battalion commander, an impressive man, the hands-on commander, a beautiful man. I remember him first of all as a teenager, thin and full of smiles, as he was barely fifteen years old when he first came to the Command Military Academy near the Reali School in Haifa. He was part of the Granite Battalion, together with my son. That is how I met Jamal and his family, the remarkable Abbas family: Lila, a loving mother and brilliant educator, head of a respected and excellent school; Colonel (Res.) Annan, a proud father and exemplary commander himself; Major (Res.) Gideon, his big brother, graduate of the Command Military Academy, an esteemed commander and an inspiration to Jamal; and his little sister, Mir'el, the apple of the family's eye. Since then, we have been in contact over the Jewish and Druze holidays, and at promotion and honorary award ceremonies—the Abbas family has provided me with a lot of work in that respect—and the men of the Abbas household are serial recipients of honorary awards. Just two weeks ago I congratulated Annan twice: first for receiving the rank of colonel and again for the rank Gideon was promoted to. If only we could continue like that. Just like that. If only we could meet in Peki'in at Jamal's wedding. But fate wanted otherwise, and on Saturday evening my heart broke upon hearing that Jamal had fallen in battle in Gaza, as commander of the 101 Battalion of the Paratroopers Brigade. On Sunday we went, Benny and I, to pay our final respects to Jamal in Peki'in, the place he was born, where his roots are, and one of the most beautiful and special places in Israel.

As Major (Res.) Nir Sabir, Commander of the Granite Battalion at the Command Military Academy, eulogized at Jamal's funeral, Jamal, that small skinny kid (at the time they thought he had lied about his age to be able to attend the boarding school), braved the challenges of the academy as well as the Reali High School. He overcame the language barrier as well as other obstacles and progressed professionally, socially, and academically, so it came as no surprise that he excelled at the academy and continued to do so in every other venture he faced, with honors and distinction. He was always so proud to be a Druze, and I remember how excited my son was after his battalion visited Peki'in. During this visit they were privileged to listen to Jamal's grandfather, retired colonel Gideon Abbas, one of the first high-ranking Druze officers in the IDF. Listening to him was like receiving a lesson on Zionism and what it means to love your homeland, a memorable lesson in following a righteous path.

We knew that Jamal's funeral would be a large one, so we decided to set out early. My son, the officer, came from his base somewhere in the south of Israel. (Deep appreciation to his commanding officer, who in spite of all the operational constraints granted him the time and effort to attend the funeral). And so we drove north during a storm, up the mountain to

Peki'in, where all the streets were adorned with Israeli and Druze flags.

We arrived about an hour before the funeral, and the Community Center was already quite full. The place was not filled with Jamal's soldiers, as they were still fighting in Gaza. But their parents came, to pay their last respects to their sons' battalion commander. A brave commander who was like a father and a leader to them. Many military personnel attended, cadets from the Command Military Academy with their team commander, a graduate of the Granite Battalion herself. Many soldiers from the Granite Battalion attended too, some of them still serving in the military, some of them reserves, a few of them civilians. Many of them could not attend due to the war, but their partners came instead. Because they are close like that—they've been together for years. And these wonderful people, young women in their early twenties who themselves have for many days had no contact with their partners fighting in Gaza, came to bid farewell to Jamal. They came, like me, parents of the Granite Battalion, who together raised this wonderful group where comradeship exists like nowhere else—it is hard to describe. Comradeship between soldiers combined with youthful mischief built over a period of three years together. Not only brothers in arms. Just plain brothers. We all stood there together, brokenhearted and sad.

On one side there was a platform where many of the Druze elders sat, in traditional dress, some of them praying. The second floor of the hall was also full. Inside the hall, in a large room, where his coffin was placed, sat row upon row of women softly singing a very sorrowful tune, almost meditative. At first, I was reluctant to enter the hall. It felt very intimate and even sacred. I realized that the top part of the coffin was open, revealing Jamal's face, but the singing of the women was what drew me inside. There was something very powerful and sad in their song. Men are also permitted to enter the hall, to bid their farewell and to pay their last respects. They come in and leave. But, as a rule, this is the women's space, and it is deeply evident. It felt like Jamal was returning to his maternal origins. To a huge womb, enveloping and absorbing. Almost like a birth. But sadly, it was just the opposite. The women's song felt painful, but also whole and all-encompassing. I went inside and looked at Jamal, beautiful, masculine in his uniform, which he loved deeply and which suited him perfectly. I fell in tears into the arms of Lila; we embraced, sobbing together by the coffin. Heart to heart. From one mother's heart to another. So much sorrow and pain. There are no words of comfort. Their song stayed with me after the funeral, and the next day I contacted friends in Peki'in, and they explained that those songs are actually wedding songs which are sung at the funeral of anyone who has died before marrying. What a touching custom. I did not take any photos at the funeral. A friend sent me a video where you can see and hear the sights and sounds from the hall.

At three o'clock the Druze/military ceremony began. From the number of photos taken by Wisam, it is evident how many people were there. (In the photos only a fraction of them can be seen. I, for example, was standing in an area that was not photographed, and behind me were still very many people). The ceremony was held in Arabic and Hebrew and comprised prayers of the Sheiks (even though I could not understand the words, I felt the gates of heaven opening), heartfelt eulogies, and laying of wreaths. On the wreath we laid, we wrote, "The parents of Granite Battalion salute you, the Command Military Academy."

From all the eulogies, Jamal's character as an outstanding officer was evident; he was determined, courageous, and daring. So was his personal character—always smiling, loving and loved, caring, and a friendly and ethical leader. All of it was true. During his service, the issue of Nationality Law arose, which Jamal had brought up to the commander in chief of the IDF. This unnecessary law humiliates the Druze, who are dedicated and sacrificial like no other. If only the Israeli government had a drop of the courage and decency of the Druze people and would cancel this abhorrent law, creating justice and equality. That is appropriate. My son, a captain in the IDF, said to me after the funeral that he feels embarrassment and shame for his friends—his Druze brothers—because of this Nationality Law. I share those feelings deeply. Our hearts are one and our country is one.

After the barrage of reverence, the ceremony ended. Only the close family members accompanied the coffin to the cemetery. As a rule, burials for the Druze are a shared family event and do not have corporeal importance. The eternal soul is what is important. However, as a gesture of respect, and due to the circumstances of death while protecting our homeland, IDF soldiers are buried in a casket, and their graves have a military headstone.

It was hard and sad to say farewell to Jamal. After the funeral we remained for about an hour, talking about him and the legacy he left, while missing him deeply.

Granite Battalion, this funeral is enough, threefold. The first, the last, and one too many. You have the duty now to protect our country. Please continue the spirit of Jamal, and as his father, Anan, said to him in their last recorded communication, stand at the spearhead of the operations, fight with bravery, reach your goals and triumph, and hopefully our troops will always, always return safely to base.

Lila, Anan, Gideon, Mir'el, and the entire Druze community, my heart is with you. We will never forget Jamal—an Israeli hero.

~

Agam Yosefzon
Agam Yosefzon, October 7

My October 7

We arrived at the party, Itamar and I, (A), (Sh), and (Al.A), at around five thirty in the morning. When we arrived, I went to talk with my friends who had come in a different car from the south. While talking with Gefen, she told me that she had been receiving many Red Alert messages from the Chamal (emergency operations room) app. All this about half an hour after we arrived. Everyone was running, trying to reach their cars, and began falling on the ground. I immediately called Itamar and asked where he was. I saw him, closed the phone, and began walking in the direction of the car. My phone, by mistake, called my mother. Without being aware of it, I woke her up, and she immediately returned my call and asked why I had called her. I said I hadn't called but that there were sirens going off, and that we were running toward the mobile shelters. I photographed the interception of the missiles and the people running away and sent it to a friend. Now I know that one of the girls I had photographed was with me in the mobile shelter. We all got back into the car and began driving toward the main road; the road north had been blocked, so we drove south. I told them that at the junction by Kibbutz Re'im there is a bus station, and next to it a mobile shelter. I thought it would be safe to wait in the shelter so we would not get injured by the rockets. Never in my life did it occur to me that terrorists would break through the fence, breaching the border.

89

We entered the shelter, and many more people came in. While we could hear the sirens we stayed inside, and when it was clear we went outside.

I thought to myself, *I can't believe that people live along the border; that they live like this on a daily basis.* There was a positive atmosphere around us; we joked about it, and then we began to hear the sounds of shooting coming from the direction of Gaza. We didn't understand what was happening. With us in the shelter there was a Muslim man from Be'er Sheva who told us that he did security work in the area. He said it seemed that terrorists had infiltrated Israel. As far as I know, he was armed. Someone came to the shelter and told us that his aunt had called him and told him to head south, as terrorists were shooting at all the cars. We understood that we needed to get inside the shelter. The shelter did not have a door; there were two wasp nests, a lot of dirt, and feces.

After a few minutes, a Nahal soldier from the Orev unit told us that he had been told by friends that terrorists had infiltrated Israel, but that everything would be okay and that they were quite far away. In addition, he said that the Re'im base was one of the largest in the country, and that we should try to stay calm. I asked him: So why are we hearing the shots so close by? He said that because they were shooting out in the open, it sounded close by. I tried to remain optimistic.

(A) messaged that they were approaching, that at the next left turn they would be turning south. We all crowded into the shelter, as many as possible. I was in the corner of the shelter, Itamar by my side. We slowly began hearing them, getting closer, talking, shooting and shouting. (A) said that if they threw grenades into the shelter, he would throw them back out, and that others should all try to do the same if he couldn't.

From the moment I heard the terrorists' voices, I sat on the floor, closed my eyes, and covered my ears. Itamar stood by my side, and someone else stood over me. Itamar asked her to get off me, as she was blocking my air. I tried stroking the back of the person in front of me, but the sounds of the terrorists were already too close; I wanted to close my ears. It was clear that something bad was about to happen. I whispered "shhhh" to myself over and over to try to calm my heart, which was pounding, and tried to remain as silent as possible. The shelter was bursting with people. We heard the terrorists approaching the entrance. Someone in the shelter said we should start reciting Shema Yisrael. After that I heard the Muslim guy going out while shouting, "I'm a Muslim, I'm a Muslim."

There were shouts, and I do not know what happened to him. The terrorists threw stun grenades and fired RPGs. Some exploded inside the shelter. (E) and others managed to throw them back out, and I said to myself, *I don't want to die, I don't want to die.* There were about eight to eleven grenades. One of the explosions made me feel a sort of death. I felt my body become a tiny creature, as if someone was folding me within myself, like I was being drawn into a black void. I could not see or hear anything but felt a kind of peace and wondered to myself, *What is wrong with this death? When will I see my whole life in front of me?* I honestly felt my body stopping. I could not feel my heartbeat. There were sounds in my head which sounded like spirits whispering things to me. I felt like I had no body; everything shrank as if it was no more. I saw and felt a large dot in my head which was moving upwards. It felt like my soul.

Suddenly, I could hear Itamar echoing in my head and saying to me, "Stay with me, stay with me."

I said, "Itamar, I am dead."

He replied, "You are not, you are here with me."

I asked him, "Can you hear me?" Breathlessly I said to him, "I cannot hold on, I'm dead." He repeated the words: "Stay with me, stay with me."

I said, "I am afraid that if I come back now, I will come back as a different person."

Itamar barely heard me saying that and just begged me to be with him, and then I felt my soul returning. I opened my eyes and could not see anything other than orange dust. Someone screamed that a girl had lost her arm. I closed my eyes again. Once again we heard terrorists approaching.

At this stage I am not sure I remember what happened first, the abductions or the shooting massacre. I think it was the abductions. They took people, dragged them, and told them to come out of the shelter. People were screaming that they did not want to and tried to fight them. They tried to talk to them in Arabic and English, to tell them "salaam." I tried as much as possible to keep a low profile. One of the girls who was taken out was then returned to the shelter by one of the terrorists, and she survived. Later on, I found out that Alon was abducted. After that, someone came inside and started shooting indiscriminately in all directions. I tried to shrink myself even smaller and play dead.

I opened my eyes again to make sure that Itamar was at my side and alive. Itamar said to me, "My love, I've been shot in the arm," and began putting pressure on the open wound without thinking twice, no matter how much it hurt him. Itamar had been hit by a bullet, which went in one side and came out the other. I was shot in the leg, but the bullet probably hit the wall or something before it hit me. I had a hole in my leg but not a large one. After that I took off all my jewelry, as I had heard something about not wearing jewelry in situations like this, but the jewelry had already burned my skin. The only piece of jewelry that remained on me was the bracelet my mother had given me when I joined the army. I forgot to remove it, as I never take it off. It too left burns on my skin, but I am glad that it remained on me.

From that moment on we tried to stay as quiet as possible so that the terrorists would not return and kill us too. Every time we heard voices outside the shelter, we put our heads under the dead bodies. I wiped the blood off my face; I took my shirt off and ripped it with my teeth. I tried to make a tourniquet for Itamar's arm, but I had no previous experience. Itamar applied pressure to the wound as much as he could. At first we thought he had only one hole in his arm, but we then realized there were two. All the while dead bodies were lying over our legs, preventing us from moving; some of them were friends, others we had just been talking and joking with moments ago.

Itamar by now could hardly hear anything in his right ear. During those hours we tried, every time we heard someone approaching, to figure out if he was entering the shelter or just walking by. We repeatedly heard terrorists approaching, talking, and laughing. The five people who were closest to the exit of the shelter had mobile reception and tried to call for help through friends and the police; they tried calling the police again and again. They said they were on their way, giving us hope, but they never came. All the while we were trying to remain as silent as possible so the terrorists would not come inside. Our legs were trapped under bodies, and I was sure that I had lost my leg. Later, after managing to move the body that was lying on top of me, I discovered I still had my leg, and what

I'd thought was a piece of my foot was actually a piece of the body lying on top of me.

After a few hours we heard a large vehicle approaching and people getting out of it. We heard ambulance sirens, and someone said, "Magen David Adom is here. You need to split into two teams and scan everything. Do not shoot recklessly at everything that moves, as they could be our people." We all agreed that we would not leave the shelter because there was a possibility that they were not really Israelis.

Moments later we began to hear shots. I don't know if it was the terrorists or the IDF shooting, but they were in the vicinity of the shelter. We waited another ten minutes, twenty minutes. Time passed slowly and no one came. We were trying to remain optimistic and to take deep breaths, to smile at one another. We had no water; the bottles we had were punctured by the shots. Both Itamar and I put pressure on his wound and stopped the flow of blood each time it began to bleed again.

After about another hour we heard someone outside say, "Bro, have you got a car?" His friend replied, "I can't find my keys," in the most perfect Israeli accent ever. We did not allow ourselves to come out of the shelter, as we were still not convinced that they were really Israelis. About twenty minutes later we heard two people speaking Arabic, probably the same two. The whole time I tried to think like a soldier—what would he do in times like this. I thought about my brother, tried to get into the heads of the terrorists, and I could find no reason that they would not return to make sure we were all dead; the whole purpose of this was to kill as many of us as possible.

After a few hours, Itamar said that he thought I was laying on his phone. I checked and found it; it was covered in blood. I wiped it clean on my clothes, but there was no mobile reception for a long time. We had no idea what was going on outside. We did not know what to do. In total ignorance of what the situation was, I was convinced that on leaving the shelter, I would find myself in an area conquered by Gaza.

Suddenly we began getting messages. Messages from worried people who thought we were safe in Tze'elim or Sa'ad according to fake news that had spread. We could not reply as we had no reception. But we still wrote messages and sent photos to Itamar's parents just in case the messages succeeded in getting through. We made sure they would know it was from us and not from Hamas. We asked the person closest to the exit to hold the phone up for a few minutes, but the messages did not go through. We tried again and again, and eventually they were sent. Many people, friends of Itamar, my friends, our families, were asking where we were and told us to send the location. It was difficult to send our location as there was such bad reception, and we could not speak over the phone as we were afraid that any terrorist outside would hear us. Others also asked us not to talk on the phone. We tried to explain that we were trying to get help. Meanwhile lots of cars were driving past all the time.

Every now and then we heard shots, booms, and Red Alert sirens. We tried to send our location to as many people as possible, what our status was and how many people we were. At some point I heard a woman shouting. I think it came from the kibbutz. I began hearing strange noises from outside, as if someone was walking by the entrance to the shelter or an animal was ripping a piece of paper to shreds; it sounded like they were dragging branches to the entrance to the shelter. I turned to Itamar and said I was afraid they were going to burn us all. Each moment became precious. After a while we saw someone holding his phone toward the inside of the shelter and removing it quickly in case there were terrorists in the shelter. After that he put his head in and asked if anyone was inside. We raised our heads and began crying. We were only seven survivors, including myself and Itamar. Itamar and I were the only wounded. The other five survivors were not physically injured, but I am sure they were mentally wounded. Those who could walked out of the shelter.

The shelter was filled with grenades and corpses, blood and body parts. The smell was awful, and flies were buzzing everywhere. We did not know if the grenades would explode, or if they had already exploded. I and another person were unable to get up. My leg was in great pain from the bullet wound. I managed to get it out from under the body lying on it but could not get up. (T)'s legs were stuck under a few corpses. I held her hand and said we were in this together and all would be okay. Meanwhile, we heard more shots outside and were afraid we were being shot at again and that we would not get out of there alive. Eli (not his real name), a civilian, and another person, a colonel, said everything would be okay. The colonel picked me up and took me to a car. I was naked from the waist up. He immediately found a towel and gave me a shirt.

When they removed us from the shelter, I did not look left or right. Only at the car. They drove us to the gas station at the Be'eri junction, where survivors and wounded had gathered. On the way I asked Eli if there was a terrorist when they arrived or if it was one of our soldiers. He said it was a terrorist. Thank goodness we did not come out when we heard them speaking Hebrew. Along the way we saw many cars with open doors and bodies lying around them. I felt like I was in a horror movie. When we arrived at the gathering site, the gas station at

Be'eri Junction, they instructed Eli to take us immediately to the Soroka Hospital.

When we arrived at Soroka, someone took a photo of me, one of the doctors and nurses there. I felt very uncomfortable about that and began shouting at her to stop photographing me. They told me it was only for identification purposes, but I did not care. Afterward they took good care of us and made sure we were okay. My arms were clenched, my fingers were stuck to each other, and my entire body trembled and shrunk from the trauma; I couldn't relax. The entire time, Itamar had defended me with his body. We hid behind and under dead bodies. Itamar kept telling me to smile, saying that everything would be alright. Itamar and I have a thing—we make pinky promises on all sorts of things we wish upon ourselves to make sure they will happen.

When this whole thing began, Itamar made me a pinky promise that we would get out of here alive, and we did not lose hope for a moment. I felt people were praying for us, but I didn't really believe that we would be found and thought that none of the rescue teams would care about us. We believed we were going to die there, without food or water. Now I am home, trying to recover from it all and to attend to the trauma I experienced. Every time I hear even the smallest boom or a car going by, and so many other things, I look around to make sure everything is as it should be and I am protected. Even now, writing my story over the last five days, every time I remember the smallest detail, my heart begins to beat at two hundred and my whole body begins to shake. All this and I am only twenty years old.

Can anyone give me a logical reason why I had to experience it all? I just want to live peacefully in my country. I will have to deal with this trauma for the rest of my life. Although usually I am very active on social media, I have never shared much personal information, or feelings, or weaknesses, but I know that it is important that the world knows what we had to go through—important for me, too, to confront and accept all that I have been through. I cannot fathom that so many days have passed since then. It feels to me like it was yesterday, but now we are surrounded by people who love us, and who are happy that we miraculously survived, together. Aner Shapira of the Orev Battalion of the Nahal saved our lives, and he deserves a medal for that; he is our guardian angel.

Itamar lost two of his close friends, and one of his friends was abducted. He had shrapnel in his face and the rest of his body and was shot in the arm; the bullet went through and came out the other side. He has already been operated on and is waiting for his next operation. Both his eardrums were torn. I have some shrapnel in my head, front and back. I have blisters on my hands and a hole in my leg from a bullet in my shoe. Much of my hair has fallen out as a result of the trauma and also from the blood and dust which clogged it all together. People who know me know how sensitive I am about my hair and can understand what that means to me. Obviously, I am grateful every moment that I am still breathing,

I have been blessed with a new life. In total we spent seven hours in the shelter, from 7:20 in the morning until 14:19, helpless, without food or water.

I wish to convey my condolences to all the families of the many victims. I hope and pray that all the hostages will be quickly returned.

Ayelet Arnin, Segev Israel Kizner—may their souls be bound in the bundle of life. RIP.

Aloni, I hope you will return quickly, healthy and whole to us and to your family and friends who love you so much; I hope that you remain optimistic and strong there.

There are many details missing from my story. I kept a lot to myself, things people do not have to know. Perhaps it is not my decision whether to tell these stories to the world. I did not see it all; I had my eyes shut for most of the time the terrorists were close by. I know it is not only my story, but also the story of the murdered, the hostages, and other survivors. This is how I saw or did not see some things.

~

Meital Yanko Genis
The Bravery of Soldiers

This is the story of Sefi and Gal's bravery.

I just received a shocking telephone call from the only survivor of the mobile shelter where Sefi and Gal hid. The first thing she said was that Sefi and Gal saved her life.

She told me that they met in the shelter near Re'im that morning after the sirens and that they were both injured by shrapnel from a rocket which fell by their car while trying to escape. They were quite frightened and waited there together with two women. At some point, they began to hear hundreds of terrorists on pickup trucks and motorcycles shooting in all directions; they also understood that the terrorists were going through all the shelters one by one, killing everybody. When the terrorists approached the shelter where they were hiding, they heard the footsteps of a terrorist coming their way. Without thinking twice, Sefi and Gal left the shelter and pounced on the terrorist, trying to prevent him from entering. They managed to delay him outside until at some point they were both shot and killed on the spot.

Afterward, more terrorists arrived and managed to enter the shelter. They threw grenades inside and shot continuously.

One girl survived the carnage. The first thing she wanted to do once she was released from the hospital was to share the story of this heroic deed.

There could be no new ending to this story, but it was important to her that we know that thanks to them, she is alive. There are so many stories that no one is alive to tell; what a privilege to hear this story. Sefi and Gal did not just sit around waiting for their turn to come, but fought unarmed until the last minute and died as heroes.

You were and will always be angels in this world as well as in the next.

~

Noa Madar
In Memory of Captain Dor Sadeh, RIP

Dori.

We parted three days before the war began. The extreme feeling of loss does not lighten, not at all.

Things ended for us on Wednesday with a bit of anger, but I had hopes that you would send a message, we would talk, maybe you'd even come home after a while, who knows.

On Saturday this dreadful war began and I sent you a message, I begged you not to make it more difficult for me, said that I understood.

Dori.

Since learning that you fell in battle, I'm so upset things ended the way they did, that our last meeting ended in both love and anger.

I hope that you are a bit less angry now and still feel love, because I do.

I thought a lot about whether you would want me to eulogize you as my partner or be angry at me for doing so. I made the choice for us both; because you were a real gentleman, you let me lead and decide. So I decided to reveal the good that was and what could have been, if only you had not been there that night at Kfar Aza.

Dori.

Suddenly everything, little things, remind me of you.

Black coffee in the morning, seriously? Why did you also have to love black coffee?

To make the bed, the first thing I do in the morning, only since I've been with you.

To eat bread with soft scrambled eggs, our regular breakfast that we never got tired of.

To blow your nose 24/7 when you had a cold; you were always carrying a soft tissue.

To pass the Dor Alon gas station on Road 6—how can I not remember you in everything I do?

Dori.

How can I go forward when you cannot? You will always be 22; I won't.

How can I watch stand-ups and *Kupa Rashit* without you?
Drink red wine
or beer.
To eat Bamba Nougat
or popcorn.

Dori.

Thank you.

Thank you for eight months of love twenty-four hours a day. Thank you for being my first grown-up relationship. Thank you for your honesty and openness.

Thank you for respecting and appreciating me.

Thank you for making me laugh and laughing with me.

That you loved me, you made sure you reminded me even when I found it hard to believe.

Thank you for making sure that I would be happy.

For good-morning messages and good-night, princess. For long telephone conversations at the end of the day.

Thank you for sending me photos of you eating the cakes I would bring to the base, even though you don't even like sweet stuff as it upsets your stomach, only so I would keep smiling.

Thank you for not being angry when I put salt in your coffee; you even laughed about it.

Even when I would kiss you with loads of Labello and you walked around with red lips without being aware of it until you looked in the mirror and laughed out loud at yourself.

Thank you for agreeing to change for me.

Thank you for fighting for us again and again.

That you loved me like no other.

You taught me a lot about love, that it comes in many shapes, not only one.

Dori.

I knew that I loved you.

But only after you were killed did I understand how much.

Dori.

Typically,

you were at the head of the group.

In your death you saved many families.

You died the death of a hero.

You will be forever twenty-two.

May your soul be bound in the bundle of life.

Dori.

I have loved.

I still love.

Will always love.

What remains is the hope that you did too.

From me for the last time, Noa, your partner.

~

Asaf Perry
A State of Superheroes

The Bible teacher is really a commando fighter,

And the kindergarten teacher is really an intelligence officer.

No one knows that the fancy high-tech neighbor is a company leader in the armored corps, and nobody noticed that the contractor with the funny hat who's building the house across the street is a combat pilot.

That the sharp-looking lawyer from the apartment upstairs grinds shifts as an operations officer in the division, and that the funny guy from the grocery store is a sniper, who right now is lying on a half-destroyed roof in Gaza.

They say that the tough bank branch manager is a deputy battalion commander in the Home Front Command at the hotels in the Sea of Galilee, and the smiley bus driver is a commander of a battery of cannons in the north, and the highly efficient interior designer is a paramedic in the West Bank.

The legend tells that the nerdy physics student is actually from the naval flotilla, doing imaginary operations, no one even knows where.

Or he's actually in the General Staff Reconnaissance Unit (Sayeret Matkal).

They look like people from the village, with regular clothes, regular jobs, and regular lives. But it's all a cover story.

Because when you suddenly need them, then they open a hidden closet, a secret drawer, or some crate under the bed, and take out their reserve magical cape and go save the world.

We look ordinary, but really—

We are a state of superheroes.

~

Amit Bar
Selfie

My love . . .

We cannot complete the picture of what happened without Ziv, and until he comes home it is not over.

But we are miraculously here.

It began with rockets. It was frightening, but I was able to comfort myself, thinking that the chances one will fall on me are slight.

Everything will be okay.

We try to drive away until we realize that everything is blocked, everyone wants to escape. So we wait for a while for things to calm down, we lay down low so as not to be hit, but then people begin running and shouting that there are terrorists.

We run, like sheep from the slaughter, we run to the fields and you hold my hand, pulling me along with you.

We hear the bullets whooshing close by. People are dropping and the fucking terrorists are chasing us, surrounding us from all sides on motorbikes, trying to murder us. When I tell you I can't run anymore, you say we have no choice, we must continue to run for our lives.

We try to hitch a ride, but you say that on foot is the safest. We are not able to escape when you, Ziv, and I separate, and we both go on to hide in the bushes. Bullets flying above our heads—I never knew till now what the whistle of a bullet sounds like. The terrorists pass us by, shooting in every direction, and we do our utmost not to move and to keep silent.

Suddenly you decide to take a selfie. I am about to get angry—why now—but you say that at least if we die, our families will have a memento of us loving each other until the very end.

You protect me with your body, and I think of all the other couples whose ending was different from ours.

The scenes there are impossible to grasp, and it is impossible to digest what we experienced. We can only continue to pray that Ziv will come back home to us.

~

Elad Avraham
I Understood Love, I Understood Hate

It has taken twenty-three days and maybe a lifetime, but here comes the long-awaited post.

Rabbi Nahman of Breslov says, "Anything in your power, do."

I decided to write this post on my birthday, October 30, as on October 7 I was reborn and received the gift of life, and many things became clear.

I understood that to go armed into an area swarming with terrorists without a safety vest is a crazy idea but one that would succeed.

I understood that God is looking out for me.

I understood that there would always be people who would want to do what I did.

I understood that there are people who are blind to evil.

I understood that I had done something larger than life.

I understood that I wanted to help.

I understood that the festival community is filled with amazing people.

I understood that Nova has become a symbol of freedom and love.

I understood who is real.

I understood that there is no such thing as justice.

I understood that the world is a crazy place where we cannot know what will happen a minute from now, and how important it is to enjoy the here and now.

I understood that some people are born to chase and others to flee.

I understood that there are Jewish superheroes.

I understood that I must do and be silent.

I understood that there are no boundaries.

I understood that there will always be those that have something to say and also understood that they will continue to flee and I will continue to chase.

I understood that I must see the good.

I understood that 90 percent of the people I saved that day will never know that.

I understood that it does not matter.

I understood how close I was to death during an entire day of fighting.

I understood that we are the chosen people.

I understood that never again is now.

I understood that to excel is imperative.

I understood love.

I understood hate.

I understood that we have to go on, for the fallen.

I understood that one must embrace one's loved ones every day.

I understood that we have no other country.

So I will not congratulate myself on my birthday, only wish that the world will become a better place. It all starts with us.

So spread love freely, be a good person.

Or at least try to be.

Do you understand?

Happy birthday to me.

~

Hottest Place in Hell Magazine
In Kissufim's War Room

Warning! This text is hard to read

Yesterday, on her way home, a young lookout who had finished her course just four days before recorded for us what she
went through on October 7 in Kissufim's war room:

At 6:30 a.m. I heard an alarm clock, I had to get up, and then
the "Tzeva Adom, Tzeva Adom" (missile alert) started. We
didn't know what we were supposed to do because we'd never
been in this situation before, so we just ran outside into this
concrete cylinder. We went inside it, but it wasn't really the
safest—the boom sounds there were just excessively so insane
that I thought I was going to die. Rockets started falling near
our residences, and shrapnel flew at us, and all the girls started
crying. Even the girls who had been there a long time said that
it was never this strong. That was only the beginning.

Messages of a raid started coming in, meaning the infiltration of terrorists into Israel . . . not only in our war room
but also in Nahal Oz, Yftah, Re'im, and Kerem Shalom. In all
the lines of communication, we heard that masses of terrorists
were coming in, and at our place someone started reporting
even before that, but the forces didn't make it on time to come
and stop them. It was an insane number of terrorists. They
started shooting at the Paskals—huge computers on stands—
and the lookouts' cameras, and so we could not observe.

They told us that our only choice was to take ourselves
and run for our lives to the war room. As the alarms went off,
rockets fell near us, and I ran like I've never run in my life. We

just ran. We went inside the war room, and they told us that everybody was abandoning their posts.

They told all of us to abandon our posts and hide behind the Paskals, just hide.

We all huddled there together, hiding, and the forces came to secure us. We had one door that couldn't close because the lock was jammed, so the crew sat on it, which was already a horrific situation, but then the terrorists cut our electricity. Both doors are electric. Once the power went out, both doors opened.

At the beginning there was a Golani team, but very quickly they all got wiped out, just died one after the other. They started bringing wounded people into the war room. I started helping treat them as much as I could because I was very scared of going out from behind the Paskals. You are just so scared for your life; it's also hard mentally.

We didn't eat for twenty-six hours. There was no food and barely any water—we shared the last few sips between all of us. We stayed like this from 6:30 a.m. till something like 11 p.m. Because the electricity was out, we had no air conditioning, no air, and we were dying of heat. I peed into a cup and a trash can twice. We had nowhere to pee in. People were shitting out of stress, girls peed their pants, things you can't even describe.

I can't even describe how scared for my life I was every second I was there. I was scared to move, scared to sit. Your body collapses. We didn't eat or drink. Nothing made sense at all. I hid inside a drawer—I lay down inside of it, scared for my life because the doors opened, and the terrorist took over the war room, and there were many dead and injured screaming at us, "My friend died, my friend died in my arms." People were coming in with a grenade exploded in their faces. What went down there was one big movie, a horrifying movie.

And then a fire alarm went off, and I felt that I was going to die, because if we went outside there were terrorists there, and if we stayed inside, I would die in the fire. Luckily, they managed to put the fire out. Apparently in Nahal Oz they burnt down the entire war room and then the girls didn't have any choice: it was go outside or stay inside and burn, so they went outside, and then it was unclear if they were kidnapped or what.

Each time the terrorists knocked on our door was so scary. We had nowhere to hide; we were in the fucking war room, the room that they were trying to get into the most. For the third time we had to beg for forces to come. So many terrorists and lots of our people dead and injured. No one knew how to act, and everybody was crying and hysterical and wanted to go home. I don't know how I survived.

They started shooting at us from the doors. In the end we managed to neutralize them, but in the second infiltration they were standing on the roof of the war room. We begged the forces to bring a Zick, a missile that would blow them away. At some point the generator started working and then stopped again, and then we started killing a lot of the terrorists who were running for their lives, and we blew them up. We saw that some kit bags of uniforms had been stolen.

They tried to get us out of there, and we were scared. There were also missiles the whole time, so we waited a little longer. In the end we stood in pairs in a line, and on both sides there were teams of soldiers protecting us, and then the shooting started when we were outside of the war room. We were the most exposed; we ducked in there, and I was sitting on other soldiers' blood because there was nowhere else to sit. By the time we reached the bus, we saw people's bodies. A lot of my other observer friends were killed. Tanks stopped working, and we were not prepared in any way.

Now every noise stresses me out, as well as every boom and every door slam or someone sneezing. I am not going back, I can't. How do I get back to my life? There is no way I can sleep alone. I can't do anything a normal person can do. It's unfair that girls our age had to go through this, and I was only on my second day there.

~

Ziv Navon
You are my song of songs (Shir HaShirim)

My husband, my handsome man, the love of my life for all my life until my dying day.

I still can't process this horrible disaster that fell upon us and changed my life.

You left with the first force with your characteristic determination. You went in on an impossible mission as a single force in a place with dozens of terrorists and fought until the last moment against this inferno with the heroism and bravery that only Ido possesses, and I know you would do it again and again to save people and our country, fighting for our home.

It was love at first sight. It was clear to me that you were the one for me in this world, and I thanked God for bringing you to me. Luckily, I told you how much I loved you every second of the day. There was no such thing as Ziv without Ido! True love that hurts my bones.

Only a week ago we were on vacation in Seychelles, planning our lives together and waiting to build our little family and put our efforts into this after so many years in the army in intensive roles for both of us. You were all my dreams coming true, I couldn't wait to see you as a dad, and I knew how lucky I was that our child would grow up to be like you—the most talented person I know, the smartest, funniest, most beautiful, someone who has values and is kind at heart. There was no one who didn't fall in love with you!

I couldn't believe that something perfect like this existed in the world!

In the end I was left alone, six months pregnant, when you died on my birthday of all days. How much can the heart take?

My heart is torn and bleeding, and I'm looking for the strength to pick myself up, but I promised you I would dedicate my life to our child, and to memorializing you. It's a child who won't get to know his incredible dad, but I will give him all the love you can possibly give so he won't feel any absence, and I will tell our child how his dad was a hero and how many people he saved. You are our pride.

I love you till the end of my life, my Ido forever. I'm not saying goodbye to you. Thank you for all the love and joy you gave me, even if it was only for a little while.

You are my song of songs, even a thousand lifetimes would have been worth it if in the end I made it to you.

~

Laura Malo
The Colombian DJ Who Was Saved from the Inferno

I've felt the need to publish something since everything happened. It's just that I wasn't able mentally . . .

So many feelings, thoughts; so much confusion—just speechless. The first pictures were taken before the terrible disaster.

Before they took our innocence and smiles.

I want to share a little of my personal experience:

It was a month ago today (feels like it was yesterday) that we managed to escape from the terrorists shooting at us.

Once the missiles started, we all lay down on the floor, panicked, waiting for the volley of missiles to lighten up a bit. When we realized it wasn't going to stop, we decided to split up. From then on it was just me and Itamar.

My intuition said we should drive south even if the route was longer. This way we could bypass the missiles and get home.

On our way we saw a mobile shelter (migunit), so we decided to protect ourselves in there. Inside were about ten people from the party and the general area (all alive, thank God!). We started hearing gunfire, but we still didn't realize the gravity of the situation until a couple of Bedouins came running to warn us of terrorists on motorcycles shooting all over!

We ran to the car as fast as we could, and while we were driving I was looking on the map for the closest place to hide . . . Kibbutz Nir Oz.

When we were nearing the yellow kibbutz gate, we saw a "soldier" right near the entrance. Everything happened in a matter of seconds. All of a sudden, I realized that the weapon was directed at us, and Itamar saw a vehicle full of bullet holes. We took a sharp turn to the left, and they were shooting at us. One bullet went through the window a few centimeters from my head.

We drove over rocks and iron rods on a winding road until the car got stuck and we drove into a fence. The fence locked us inside the car, I kicked the window with the bullet holes, and we jumped out through it.

We ran for our lives, not knowing if the terrorist was behind us or if there were other ones waiting on the other side. Me and Itamar found ourselves lying in an abandoned and dirty greenhouse while fire ants and spiders climbed all over us. Every breath was noise . . . and in the meantime, shots were flying all over, missiles and screams . . . We lay there without any means of protecting ourselves or understanding what the fuck was happening! How was it already 7:00 a.m., and a minute ago we were dancing and laughing? How the hell had we found ourselves in this situation?

Without thinking twice, I went into my contacts and called my parents. I wanted to say goodbye while I still could . . .

I had no time and no battery.

My father picked up. I briefly explained to him what was happening, and he just fell apart, crying (I never heard my father cry). My parents stayed on the other side of the phone, praying and begging God to protect us, not take us.

That was the scariest moment of my life. It's not every day you accept your own death . . .

Among all the crying and silence without being able to make even a small sound, I heard my father's voice in the background while I was lying there. I felt my life go by in a flash like a movie: My family, all my friends, all the memories, all my dreams of being the great DJ I always dreamt of being, I saw everything fall apart before my eyes.

I was ready to hang up on my parents in case a terrorist came.

Just don't let them hear how their little girl is being murdered.

It was sixteen hours of fear, sixteen hours of uncertainty, but in those hours, I prayed to God for hours on end. I want to thank Him that I am here to tell you that today, a month ago, I was reborn. God gave me a second chance at life, and my life is a miracle from above!

I want to tell everybody that we are not alone, that we are stronger than anything, and that the scars may stay, but I hope that the open wound may someday heal. We need to say thank you for every day we are alive. Every day that passes we get our life as a gift, and we need to protect what we have.

We won't forget and won't forgive, but we won't put our heads down and won't break against anybody!

Thank you to anyone who has read this far.

To anyone who gave their share and helped while we were in danger, thank you for all the concern, while we were there and also after. Thank you, Itamar—I already told you, you are the angel that God sent me!

~

Elyasaf Ezra
Wingless Angel

Pray for him.

He hasn't slept in two weeks, because when he closes his eyes, he has nightmares. The sights he saw are sights that would soften even the toughest of eyes. With the tears he cried you could build an ocean of tears.

Meet Moti Bukchin, ZAKA Search and Rescue's spokesman, who has been volunteering for this organization of angels for twenty-eight years. Week after week, day after day, he volunteers to do what nobody else wants to do.

For twenty-eight years he has made sure that a mother who's lost what's most precious to her will have a grave to cry on and a body to see for the last time.

Last night this wingless angel collapsed in his home and was hospitalized. For two weeks before this, Moti moved from horror scene to horror scene, home to home, body to body. Even his great kind heart couldn't withstand the size of this evil, and he just collapsed.

Hamas not only destroyed bodies, they destroyed souls as well.

Pray for him, please—for him and for all the ZAKA volunteers, our soldiers, and all who see and do—for them to go in peace and return in peace, healthy and sound, in body but also in soul.

~

Avigail de Garcia
Dor Mangdi—a Hero of Israel

On Saturday morning, we woke up panicked, thinking you'd be late for work, and then you were called (for reserve duty), and you said I should watch the videos they began distributing.

In five minutes, they'd already come to pick you up. You went to the car and then came back to give me a kiss and a hug because you never forgot.

You said you were going to your squad and then took a shielded vehicle. I didn't understand how big the disaster was in that moment, and I'm sure you didn't either. You were always so calm and optimistic, with a smile that won everyone's hearts.

You told me you were on your way to Ofakim. I asked if everything was alright, and you said yes, that you were in Ashkelon receiving your missions. You didn't tell me that by then you had already fought those scums.

At 2:40 p.m. I sent you a text asking if you were okay, and you didn't answer anymore . . .

My Luli,

We met three years ago, but apparently it wasn't the right time for us then . . . and I was lucky enough for you to come back into my life for ten short months. Even in my dreams, I couldn't imagine how good they'd be.

From day one we always knew that this was forever. You always said that on our one-year anniversary you were going to propose. You were more eager to get married than I was. Your biggest dream was to get married and bring a little Dor into our lives.

Honey, you made sure to remind me every night that you've had love in your life before, but never love like mine, and that you'd never give up on me. You always said that no matter what we were going through during the day, we would never go to sleep unless both of us were smiling, and we only fell asleep after the hug-and-kiss-goodnight ceremony.

Luli, you were my first love, my old love, my first kiss, the person who taught me what love really is, who taught me how to show feelings, my best friend, the partner I had always been waiting for, the only person who could contain me and understand me. Even without talking, you knew exactly what I was going through and how to operate in any situation so that I would feel the best in the world.

You gave me ten months where every morning I'd wake up happier and loving you more.

Every day I made sure to remind everybody I knew that I had the perfect partner, and my eyes would shine when I talked about you.

Everyone who knew us said we were the same person in male and female form, but I know you were a few levels ahead of me.

Everyone who knows Dor knows that he had an unusual love for himself. There was one sentence you said to me the first week we were together: "One day I will love you more than I love myself."

How I waited for you to say it to me, but you always said you were not a man of words, you were a man of actions, and that you didn't have to speak for me to know how much you loved me. Every time I was surprised to find out how much you really meant that sentence and how you'd implement your love in actions and not just words.

~

Netanel Elinson
The Secret of Unity

I wholeheartedly believe in the wonders we are about to get to see up close.

Look,

We all understand we are dealing here with the Iranian-Persian octopus trying to send its arm from India to Kush.

And the last time that the Persian kingdom tried to destroy us all, they did it in a moment of a huge separation, and what was it that brought them down?

Check it:

The Book of Esther describes how the mighty Persian kingdom is taken over by the forces of Haman, whose aim is nothing short of the final solution:

"Destroy, kill, and lose all Jews, from young boy to old people, infants and women in one day."

This is the moment the evil Haman decides on his plan:

"There is one nation scattered and divided."

Jews are scattered in all of the nations. But it's not just a geographic separation. Haman says: The Jews are divided and not united. They are at the peak of their weakness; this is the moment to hurt them.

Haman the Amalekite, the absolute evil, is great at finding moments of fraction and weakness, like a shark smelling blood. There is no need to describe here the entire story of the book, but the distinct moment where the transformation happens in the book is where Esther tells Mordechai the following words:

"Go gather all the Jews."

Esther asks for unity from all the Jews. For them to pray for her together. To be with her in her mission.

The Jews unite, and from that moment on, the book goes on at a rapid pace to reveal a complete reversal.

From a real existential threat to the entire Jewish nation to bringing judgment to all of those who seek to do us wrong:

"Let it be revered for the Jews to rule over their haters."

Persia—Iran—almost managed to destroy us when we were divided, but in a moment of great unity the decree was reversed.

And alongside training and reserve duty and preparation so that we will never be complacent again, alongside all of this I look at our situation as one of fate.

Even now our enemy helps us see his aim. When the Iranian regime is putting in huge efforts, using fake profiles online whose entire purpose is to sow separation and hate, you realize that for us this is a key point.

And so you should know that if you're contributing societal divisions and spreading greed and filth, you're just fanning the flames of our enemy.

I'm not talking about lessons learned or insights, but about people still talking the toxic talk that was here up until Simchat Torah.

And since we are lucky enough to witness this great unity, one like I have never seen since I could think for myself, I am full of faith that the second Purim miracle against the kingdom of Persia and her metastases has already begun taking shape.

What's happening here among the tribes of the Jewish nation, as we emerge from the great tear we experienced, is inconceivable. We get to see not only unity of rhetoric or shared faith, but how each faction manages to see not the downsides of the other tribes but their strengths. Most of what's happening now in the nation of Israel is an eye from which we get to see our friends' virtues and not their defects. This is the supreme unity.

When I told those insights to Neta, my love, I told her: But we don't have time to wait until Purim . . . we'd better see the salvation in Heshvan (October and November).

And she said:

Indeed! That the bitter month of Heshvan will turn high—Heshvan

From bitter to high

Amen Amen Amen

~

The Zionist Leadership Fund
Doesn't Fall Short of the 1947 (Tashach) Generation

Aner Elyakim Shapira, twenty-two years old, from Jerusalem:

A month ago on a Saturday night, the entire Shapira family got together for a holiday feast. The dinner was exceptionally pleasant, and father Moshe and mother Shira repeatedly told their children how much they enjoyed being with them.

After dinner the oldest son, Aner, a fighter and a commander in the Raven Battalion of the Nahal Brigade, left for a nature party in Re'im.

Even though him being a warrior was an obvious outcome of the Zionist value-based education he received at home, it wasn't a dominant part of his personality.

In fact, it was far from it. Aner loved Jerusalem, loved Hapoel Jerusalem (soccer team), and above all was a piano player, a gifted musician successfully starting his way.

In the last recording of Aner in the early morning at the party in Re'im, one hour before the attack started, we can see a guy in his most comfortable and natural state. Having fun and surrounded by friends, nature, and of course music.

When the attack started, he was called to come back to his base, and he left straightaway, while calling his soldiers to come.

An alarm (Tzeva Adom) going off while he was on the road led him into a portable shelter which already contained thirty young, scared people who ran away from the party, huddled together.

In one second Aner turned from a party man into a fighter and a commander. He calmed everybody down and gave them confidence.

When the sounds of gunfire and screams came near the

portable shelter, he realized what was going to happen. He turned to his brothers and sisters in fate and told them: the terrorists are about to throw hand grenades into the portable shelter. I'm going to stand in front, near the entrance, and throw the grenades back. If I get hurt or don't succeed, you do the same.

And so it was.

First grenade thrown, Aner caught it and threw it back at the terrorists.

And then a second grenade.

And a third.

And a fourth and a fifth and a sixth and a seventh.

And so it went on for a few unthinkable, unimaginable minutes in which Aner Shapira led with his bare hands a heroic battle against a heavily armed group of terrorists.

The eighth grenade blew up in his hands.

After that the terrorists also fired an RPG into the portable shelter and killed and kidnapped many of its inhabitants.

But eight of them were saved, and because the other bodies took most of the shrapnel, they only were lightly injured.

"The soldier," said the survivors to their rescuers, "he saved us. Thanks to him we are alive. He stood at the entrance very bravely and threw all the grenades back at them."

Eight hand grenades and one charming young man.

"Aner loved people" said his father, Moshe. "He loved life and sought justice.

"He came from music and loved music but never forgot the values of dedication, fraternity, and friendship. This is how we would like to remember him."

In his memory.

~

Almog Boker
Forgiveness!

I'm reading your messages over and over, your cry for help, the last message before the terrorists came inside your house and that was it—reading the messages of those I responded to, of those whose locations I sent to the forces in the Gaza Envelope; of those I couldn't manage to send to anybody; and of those whose messages I missed.

Hundreds of texts, one after the other, and I tried, but not enough.

I've been feeling guilty for thirty days.

Trying to figure out if there was something I could have done to save another one, one more of you, if it was right to broadcast your screaming pain, or if I should have broadcasted less and applied more pressure to the forces in the field. Maybe I could have sent another hero to save you.

Thirty days of endless anguish, a burning desire to go back to that morning and try something else. Thinking about Yaniv's final seconds when he was sure until the last moment that the army was going to get to him, and about Shahar, and Roee and Smadar and Gil and Ofir, and the list is so long and never-ending. I'm thinking about your children, and I see the faces of my children there, and I can't stop crying. Emptied.

I'm trying to find consolation in those that were saved—in the children in Geula whose location I sent and who were extracted; in the little girl extracted from the inferno thanks to the chilling text that her family member sent me; in Michal, who by an unbelievable coincidence was not far from a police officer who went in under fire while talking to me on the phone to extract her.

But I feel empty and guilty for those who weren't.

I want to tell you, each and every one of you, that I don't fall asleep at night before I think about you a little bit. I read your messages again and again. I'm trying to remind myself of the good things and fall asleep with a smile.

I try and fail.

I am asking for your forgiveness that I didn't do enough, but I promise you I will not stop screaming until your brothers, your children, your friends are brought back from Hamas captivity. And I promise you one more thing: that forever I will do anything, anything I can, so that your families, ours, will get to live safely.

I love you and I ask for your forgiveness

~

Shoham Nuriel
An Angel Stayed Back to Keep Ziv and Lin Safe, and the Three of Them Never Came Back.

Liel, Ya Liel, my brother, there are no words to describe the love we had. Sitting here writing about you wasn't in our plans, my brother. You are a part of me, a part of my heart and soul. Today when you went away, half of me went away with you, and half of you is still with me. Everybody who saw us for the first time couldn't understand the connection we had—two crazy people fighting all day, but a second later it's like nothing happened, sitting there, laughing and having fun.

Our connection was special, something no one else had, always the center of attention no matter where we were.

Two people completing each other. Soulmates. Wherever you went, I followed, and wherever I went, you came with me—all day every day in each other's ass, from sitting with friends, parties, driving to games when we got drafted, up until our big trip together, everything together

Everything I went through in the last seven years was with you.

Partners in everything, arriving everywhere together because that's how it was.

"Soham and Liel" is a stage name.

From the day we met we instantly became best friends, and the rest is history. We planned our entire lives ahead, how we'd live next to each other and get crazy rich, and we'd take on the world, and our kids would be best friends just like us, continuing our way.

And now you're gone, my brother. Where are you, calling me from the moment you wake up till the moment you go to sleep, from morning till night, one long conversation of us talking nonsense, sitting for hours, just laughing without doing anything? Who am I going to call and talk about all the bullshit I'm dealing with and what I'm going through, or just piss you off because it's funny?

I want to say thank you for everything, my brother. For being there for me in my hardest moment and also the most beautiful.

Thank you for sharing my life with me.

You are a special child—the smartest person in the world who can be the most idiotic when he wants to. A pure soul with a heart of gold who always gives all of himself—and I know that it was so in your final moments.

Your smile and laughter will be with me my entire life.

Thank you for all you taught me, my brother. I promise I will continue in your way. You are in my heart always.

I love you, my brother, and my heart is torn that you are not here with me.

Ya Booya, I don't know how my life continues without you here. I honestly don't know what to do from here. I'm empty.

There's no one who can take your place. You are the most precious person in the world to me, my brother, my everything. There are no substitutions for you and never will be.

Thank you for everything, Liel. Sometime we'll meet up there. Save me a seat next to you, Ya Booya.

We are blood brothers. I'm always with you.

~

Liza Ben David
My Taira

Remember how when you were little, I called you Tairon? A little light turning big?

You are as your name says, a child of light, with a smile you can see for miles and a presence that's hard to hide.

How much serenity you brought home. Mom always used to say that you basically raised yourself—such a comfortable child.

The friendliest child there is, one who could connect and adapt easily everywhere, took every situation lightly and maturely. You were motivated. You chose something and then you went, no time to waste, never giving up on yourself.

How was it you were always the one stabilizing and calming us down, and we were the nervous ones?

And your kindness, how kind. There is no way you would pass someone who needed help and not stop. You'd turn the world upside down trying to help and also take it into your beautiful heart.

You, just like Hodaya, had just started refining your beautiful little dreams and turning them into a reality. You started learning something that interested you just a few weeks ago. Just this last Friday, Dad bought a lamp for your business, and it is still sitting unopened on the stairs back home because you didn't even get the chance to open it.

My Tairoosh, I can't believe you are no longer mine but everybody's. I can't believe I won't get to marry you off and be happy with you for all the milestones and your success in life.

I can't believe you are no longer here for my children, who love you so much.

131

How is it that not long ago, I wrote to you in our group chat about how proud I am of us, each finding our way in life, and that we are starting to bloom. We were fantasizing about how we'd fly to Eden and bloom there.

And I am left with the fantasies because sons of iniquity trampled them for me.

Last Saturday we had a chance to talk before the alerts started next to you. You gave me a good, optimistic feeling. I asked if I should come and get you, and you said that you were doing okay and that we'd talk later. Nothing in life prepared me for what would happen a short while after that. For all that would happen the following week.

And for what's happening now, while you and I were supposed to go to a concert.

How did life turn on us like that, Tair?

Shine on us from above, show us the way, guard us, my little one.

Go shine now, like the sun. You have wings; fly far away. That's the tattoo you wanted to get and never got the chance. And now you really have wings.

And I need to let you go.

I love you with all my heart.

I'm sorry we were cut short,

Your big sister

~

Liza Ben David
My Hody

Don't go, ray of sunshine.

Everywhere you went over the years, there wasn't anyone who wasn't drawn to you, to your spice, to how you knew who you were and your worth, and wouldn't give up.

You would bond with people everywhere, from the restaurant table you were sitting at to the shoe store you were working in.

Mommy and Daddy's girl, how you cared for them and took care of them. Every day you would call and ask, *Have you eaten? Did you drink?*

Wouldn't let go of them for a moment.

A girl with big dreams that you'd only just started fulfilling. You'd only just started to reap your rewards, and people would fall in love with you even at that stage.

Your schedule had just started filling up. You opened a business, and you could start thinking about your next goal.

How can I accept that you went to that party and never came back? How much evil is there in this world? For a person who did nothing but good her whole life?

My saint, what was it you always said that made us laugh? "I will end up a rabbi, you will see."

Only two months ago you helped someone you didn't know, an older man, Arab, who was stuck in some parking lot without his wallet, and they wouldn't let him leave without paying. You said it didn't matter what ethnicity he was, and you couldn't see someone in pain like this.

So many more stories I can tell, so many experiences. Who you were for me, for Gilad and the children. Who I would turn to for every question or consultation. You were always the first person I'd go to. Who am I going to go to now?

I can't believe I have to let you go, my beautiful.

Watch over Mom and Dad, watch over us, give me strength. Give us signs of the ray of sunshine you are.

I love you, my soulmate.

I'm sorry we got cut short.

I love you,
Your older sister

~

Shelly Levaton Barel
A Glimpse into Hell

I was in Nova.

My husband, Yoav, and I had set up our booth there, celebrating our seventh wedding anniversary.

The night before, we had been part of the UNITY Festival with our sales booth, leading into the Nova Festival.

For about thirty hours, we went without sleep.

In the early morning, the sky lit up with explosions, and loud booms resonated constantly—a steady stream of aerial fire. I hadn't watched or followed the news for years; I couldn't understand why Yoav didn't tell me about the tensions in the south. Only later did I realize how sudden it all was.

It felt like a scene from a horror movie. I was utterly terrified. We sat on the floor, waiting for the nightmare to end, but it continued. The passage of time seemed irrelevant as fear gripped me, and I feared a missile would strike right there.

I told Yoav that we needed to pack up and get out. We started gathering the gear in a frenzy and cramming everything into the car—jewelry, stands, and clothes were hastily thrown into bags.

A booth that usually took half an hour to dismantle was folded in less than ten minutes.

Squeezed into the passenger seat with our gear, we headed for the exit just five minutes before the terrorists stormed the party area.

As we drove toward Be'eri, a huge traffic jam formed, as if the entire party was escaping in that direction.

Making a life-saving decision, we turned right instead. After ten minutes, the terrorists who came from the direction of Be'eri slaughtered everyone in that jam.

I am not sure why we chose that route—perhaps an instinct to keep moving.

We continued driving forward until we encountered cars on both sides of the road and people lying on the floor, not moving. Yoav told me to close my eyes and quickly made a U-turn, and we took off.

I thought it was a car accident because of people speeding out of fear of the explosions overhead, but Yoav told me it was something much bigger.

Two minutes later, an update was sent in his army unit group chat that there was an infiltration of terrorists, and it was already clear that now, in addition to rockets, we had to run away from terrorists as well.

The Waze navigation didn't work and we followed the signs. We decided to turn toward Ofakim. The road was difficult to follow, and the terrain was completely open. The shooting continued nonstop, and the booms got stronger. One boom almost knocked over our car. We were speeding at 150 km/h, full throttle straight ahead and a low gear when turning.

I was afraid that every car behind us was a terrorist.

With each car that passed us I was afraid I would be shot through the window.

In the end we reached populated areas, and from there, home. Still can't grasp the magnitude of the event and comprehend how much intuition and luck guided us yesterday.

Don't want to think about what might have happened if, but can't stop thinking about it.

How would our children grow up without us if we were kidnapped or dead.

On the night of the party, Yoav and I had talked about death, which is not the end, that there are reincarnations that mankind goes through.

In the open field I reminded him of this, and asked if it was time to say I love you.

We didn't say.

Arrived home and found out about the kidnapped and the dead. We were in shock.

So many friends, acquaintances, girls who purchased from the booth; it's unthinkable.

Girls I dressed the night before were missing, kidnapped, or murdered.

How many mourning notices will be posted on Facebook now? How many funerals and Shivas will we go to?

We survived the massacre.

But the trauma will accompany us all our lives.

~

Elyasaf Ezra
Kaddish

Instead of reading from the Torah, he said Kaddish.

Instead of celebrating his Bar Mitzvah, little Ariel, soon to turn thirteen, buried his whole family and said the Kaddish for his father, Yaniv; for his mother, Yasmin; and for his two sisters, Tchelet and Keshet.

He is the only survivor from the hell that Hamas built that day. He is the only one that survived from the house that Hamas destroyed that day.

A thirteen-year-old boy who buried his whole family.

No solace, no forgiveness, no compassion.

Even if we win, we lost.

Nothing will bring back Yaniv, Yasmin, Tchelet, and Keshet.

They won't be with him when he enlists, they won't be with him when he stands under the huppah, they won't be waiting for him outside the delivery room, they won't be with him in all the moments where family should be.

The sons of the devil took that from him, from him and from thousands more, families.

Ariel, you have a new family that includes millions of people. A family called Am Israel.

When you bring children into the world, we will be there.

That will be your victory, that will be the victory of all of us.

We love you!

~

Toha Hava Pappenheim
Hide and Seek

Mommy promised me that we would go to Anna Zeke's concert. I love Anna so much and love to dance to the songs and make TikTok videos.

I also love Noa Kirel and can't wait to see her at this year's festival. She is really, really stunning. I even managed to copy her steps in the song "The Crazy Dance."

On Wednesday, Mommy asked Daddy to buy flour so that we could bake a cake together. He came and stroked my head and said, "This flour is for my princess, so she can make us the best cake in the world," and it was funny because Daddy knows that Mommy really bakes and I just help her roll the dough.

On Sukkot, Daddy built a sukkah in the yard. He tied the white cloth around the sukkah, and Mommy bought decorations. "Mika, decorate the sukkah for us too," she asked me, and I cut colored strips and linked them together, making a long, long chain, until Mommy and Daddy laughed that for a chain that long you need a sukkah the size of our entire Kibbutz Holit, and they told me that I am talented and the most beautiful in the world, and that with a sukkah so beautiful maybe the singer Eliad would truly visit.

On Saturday morning, Mommy and Daddy appeared in the safe room where I was sleeping.

There was a "Color Red" alert. Daddy yawned and Mommy stuck a clip in her hair, took the phone, and said to him in a panicked tone, "Did you read what they're writing in the WhatsApp group?" She handed him the phone; his face lost all its color.

My Niko started barking in the living room, and a few minutes later there were knocks on the outside walls, sounds of gunshots outside, shouts in Arabic, loud knocks on the door. "Iftah, iftah al Bab," they screamed outside, Mommy held my hand and started shaking.

"Mika, quickly go up to the second floor, enter the closet inside our room, and don't move, be quiet. If you are really quiet, I promise that when this is over, I will take you to any show you want," she whispered to me. Fear filled my body. "Mika, go upstairs and take the phone with you." Daddy also asked me to "Hurry up!" I'd never seen Daddy like this. My dad is the strongest in the world.

I quickly ran up the stairs. Niko chased me but came out of the safe room, and I called him, called him, "Niko, come here."

I opened the closet door and sat inside. It was dark, I could barely move inside, and suddenly I heard gunshots and shouts: "Allah Akbar." Niko made a crying sound like he'd made when he was a puppy and wanted me to pick him up on the bed at night. Mommy shouted, "No, Gadi, no," and then I heard another gunshot.

I was shaking inside the closet, but I was quiet and hardly breathing. Then I heard the door to Mom and Dad's bedroom open, I held my breath like when Dad taught me to dive in the pool. I quietly held my breath and the door closed.

I heard things falling on the floor, glasses breaking, sounds of glass breaking everywhere.

A few minutes after that there was silence in the house. I called our neighbors on the phone and spoke quietly, and a few minutes after that the neighbor Roni arrived. He opened the bedroom and said to me in Hebrew in a soothing voice, "Mika, it's me, don't be afraid. Let's get out of here."

He opened the closet door quickly, lifted me onto his shoulders, and started running down the stairs. When we reached the last step I saw Niko bleeding, lying still on the floor. I shouted from inside, "Niko!" But Roni asked me to be quiet, so I didn't make a sound, and as we moved toward the entrance, I suddenly saw father and mother lying on the floor, bleeding, still. My heart screamed "Mommy," "Daddy," but I kept silent. I only managed to whisper "Thank you, Roni."

At the funeral, I looked at the graves of my father and mother. I saw the wrapped bodies and how they were lowered into the earth's belly, and in the silence that fell, between Grandmother's screams and cries, I didn't want a toy, not a game, not a Barbie, not a Playmobil like I used to like, not slime, not anything. I just wanted Daddy and Mommy, who would put their hands on my eyes from behind and suddenly appear in front of me, hug and kiss, caress my head, and tell me, "Mika, it was all a dark dream. It's not true at all. Remember we promised that when it's all over, we'll take you to any show you want? Go get dressed in your most beautiful dress, because the festival will start soon, and we bought you tickets very close to Noa and Anna, and we will even try to get you a selfie with them."

◆ ◆ ◆

I wrote this narrative post in memory of Meir and Liz Elharar on October 14th, who were murdered in Kibbutz Hulit. I learned of their story last night on Channel 12 News.

◆ ◆ ◆

141

My praise and honor go also to Gideon and Naama Kobani who, thanks to God's mercy and their resourcefulness and courage, rescued their daughter Adi Elharar, who was hiding in a closet, and thus her life was saved.

Living and walking testimony to the horror. Holocaust survivor Israel. An orphan, only seven years old.

~

Sigal Rozolio
As Long As Someone Remembers Me, I'm Alive

What a black morning . . .

How do you contain all this sadness? And why?

Our dear Yogev Aharon, you were like a mature brother to me, a welcome and loved family member, and like a son you were in our family, accompanying my son Yarom and his best friend from the farmers' middle school.

Just a week ago, I saw you on Saturday evening, sitting as usual with your best friend. Two soldiers with a few hours of togetherness before returning to the base and the reality of being soldiers. Who would have thought that this would be the last time I would see you?

I'm sorry I didn't say goodbye properly . . . Even when I sent a message and you didn't answer, I thought maybe you were injured, maybe you managed to escape, because I knew you; you put up a fight . . . But the heart couldn't control itself, and for many days we lived in pain, and now the worst of all has happened. Holding on to hope and praying with your family that everything is a mistake . . .

My heart aches, and there are not enough words to comfort your dear mother, Nechama, and your brothers, who only ten months ago lost their late father.

We are here, I promise you, and we will help the family with whatever they need.

You will forever remain in our hearts a hero, an angel. Watch over your family from above.

We were privileged to know you, a good soul; may you rest in peace. "A hero of the world, a boy with a smile of angels."

Yogev, God avenge his blood.

~

Dana Varon
Enough Is Enough. I Wish . . .

Simchat Torah (Torah's happiness). This year she is not happy with us, and we are not with her. This year there was sadness of Torah, as well as the price of that sadness, and there was and still is a gaping chasm.

There's an abyss in my heart and I'm afraid to look and check how deep it is. Every time the terrified faces of my brothers in the south on scooters and trucks come to my mind, I repress them, and it's hard for me to think and not think, what the hell I would do? And how did it happen? And why did it happen? And above all, will they return? Will we all return, or will another scarred and bloody event join the convoy along with Tarpat* events and other pogroms and disasters known to the suffering Jewish people.

Will we go back to what we were? What for a long time we cannot manage to be? The doubts poke into a dark and closed place in my heart that I'm afraid to give a name and a place. Because the images are back. The images of children hiding in closets, of women being loaded onto trucks without knowing where, and limp bodies without any grain of Jewish resistance. Submitted. Of my brothers. Not long ago and not the Holocaust. Here in the land of our beloved forefathers. 2023. And this helplessness winked at us and pushed into our mouth something we didn't want to taste. And told us, you know, nothing is taken for granted, not the security, not the complacency, not the place, not the satiety. Everything can be taken. Everything around you is buzzing and whispering hate. You are a sheep among seventy wolves. Hungry. Enemies. And they have no idea who you voted for. Whether you are in favor of or against the reform, and whether you fasted or prayed together or separately on Yom Kippur. Blood is blood, and your Jewish blood is the target. And together with this shadow that has no name that opened up inside my heart from this sad Simchat Torah, also comes a huge abundance from all the small, miserable, and stupid wars that have been our lot here in the last year.

Enough already. Just enough and enough.

I wish.

*Tarpat refers to the 1929 Hebron Riots

~

Netanel Alinson
Sukkah of Peace

The verse that has been with me since the beginning of the war:

> . . . That He will hide me in His tabernacle on
> the day of calamity; He will conceal me in the
> secrecy of His tent; He will lift me up on a
> rock (Psalms 27).

On Simchat Torah I left home in a frenzy from my sukkah together with hundreds of thousands of reserve soldiers. It is customary in the "Nohag Olam" that on the last day of Simchat Torah you dismantle the sukkah, but in our house, the sukkah has remained standing in its full glory since then. Our house in the Aravah is very small, and the sukkah that still stands expands the house and the soul.

I feel that there is a strong, deep symbolism. I left the house after seven days with my family. Nothing compares to that. The children and I slept in the sukkah, crowded and glued together like olive tree seeds.

Even now, my family still eats on Saturdays and during the week in the sukkah, as the desert air cools, and the sukkah keeps them from harm, and continues to offer warmth and togetherness even deep, deep in the month of Heshvan.

Thousands of sukkahs are still standing all over Israel, strangely providing me with a sense of comfort; they still carry the same aura of honor. There was a difficult "Hester Panim," but now, under the protection of the sukkah, we are safe from harm.

We recited the chapter from Psalms for forty days, until the beginning of the war. The chapter ends with the following words:

> Do not give me a troubled soul, because false witnesses have arisen in me and conspire with Hamas. If I hadn't believed to see the goodness of Jehovah in the land of the living (Psalms 27).

And yet another story from the last day of routine in our sukkah, just before the terrible Hester Panim.

It is customary to have a farewell meal from the sukkah. And this year we had a particularly sweet farewell feast.

I had just returned from studying on the night of Hosanna Raba in the center area. It was already two in the morning, and the road to the Aravah still lay ahead. As I was fatigued from the drive, I stopped to spend the night in the desert land near Be'er Sheva. This is how on the morning of Hosanna Raba I ended up at a bakery in Dimona, and behold, my eyes lit up: there were sweet jam donuts in the bakery!

I arrived at the sukkah in our home, and with great excitement I told the children that this year we would have a special meal to say farewell to the sukkah. The children jumped for joy, and at midnight we sat down to eat on the last day of Sukkot: sweet doughnuts!

I told the children at that meal that it is a great privilege to combine these two holidays, and that we are extending Sukkot until Hanukkah.

That's what I said.

Rosh Chodesh Kislev is coming soon, and it looks like my beloved family will indeed be sitting in the sukkah this year on Hanukkah and eating donuts. These two holidays are linked. Eight days versus eight days. The lulav has become a sword from Maccabi, the colorful decorations touch the light of the Hanukkah candles, and the smell of the myrtle mixes with the sweetness of the jam.

> . . . For in the day of trouble He will hide me
> in His shelter; He will conceal me under the
> cover of His tent; He will set me high upon a
> rock. Then my head will be held high above
> my enemies around me. At His tabernacle I
> will offer sacrifices with shouts of joy; I will
> sing and make music to Jehovah (Psalms 27).

The holiday of Sukkot and the holiday of the dedication of the altar and the light of the menorah are linked this year.

> Merciful Father,
> We are active and trying very hard,
>   please,
> shine your face upon us,
> Become a stronghold and a fortress, wrap us in the
>   sukkah of your peace.

~

Sigal Tzur
The Light That Went Out

My boy, my little boy, my elder son, our dessert . . .

Today, as always throughout your life, I accompanied you, but this time on your last journey. The heart contracts again and again, the pain does not let up, and the breaths are strained . . .

It was important to me that you take the last road from your beloved home, from the paths you walked all your life to kindergarten, to school, to soccer, to friends. But this time you were accompanied on your way by a large crowd of people wrapped in flags, wrapping and comforting you and us. So moving, testifying to and showing who you are, the beloved of the covenant that you were, and so worthy of you, our hero.

You joined the circle of life and illuminated it for us in unique moments.

A beautiful baby, easy to raise and calm. You never stopped smiling.

Since you were born, I felt like I lived you. You lived inside me.

Befitting the third and youngest of the family, you developed at your own pace, you had your own rich inner world. Late bloomer, they tended to say about you, and indeed you blossomed slowly, opening and slowly revealing yourself like a flower in its beauty.

In the last few years you reached your peak. I stood in awe in front of my little boy, who became a young man, with unusual physical and mental strength, containing and embracing us.

Along with your gentle and quiet temperament, from the

150

dawn of your childhood you always knew what you wanted and what you didn't. I was stunned by the quiet assertiveness that was inherent in you. You always knew what you wanted, where you wanted to be, and what didn't suit you.

I, as your mother, always listened to you at every age and stage; even the recommendations of educators we met at key intersections were different. I listened to you and understood the importance of your choices. I knew that they were what would ultimately shape your personality and your self-confidence. And indeed you have proven yourself time and time again.

You were always different. Contemporary but deprived of the Israeli audacity found in your peers. An abundant soul that radiated all around. You had a lot of modesty, respect for others, compassion, and generosity. You were full of warmth, and you were endowed with an unusual level of sensitivity for humans and animals. You often understood situations intuitively, without words, and acted in a quiet way that characterized you. You were always a child of actions rather than words.

The beloved child of mankind that conquers and charms everyone around you.

Your teachers, your commanders, and your many friends from all walks of life can testify to this. Our home has always been the place for social gatherings. How much you loved hosting, doing, buying a new projector, a screen that would project the Real Madrid football game and make the experience perfect. As we said once before, a child of silent action. You discover over time how much your little boy is a leader, and a leader in his own way.

Your last stop was the army (how terrible that sounds after speaking of the life plans you have woven). You didn't choose the easy way here either; you wanted to continue the family tradition. And despite the difficulties—and the possibilities of choosing a less demanding and dangerous route—you insisted on ending up as a warrior. The last moments of your life testify to this; you chose to get out of the jeep that was shot, continue to fight against the terrorist squads that infiltrated, and in the process divert the fire from your injured friends. How heroic, my child. I salute you for your determination, courage, and bravery. Indeed, you never stopped surprising me at any point in your life. Even in your last moments.

From the time we heard about the incident and as the hours ticked by, I felt my heart being squeezed harder and harder until it was hard for me to breathe. Every knock on the door made us jump, quickened our pulse, but when it came— we weren't ready. My Adidush, I who protected you all my life, I could not protect you in your last hours. You always trusted me. I'm sorry, my little one, that I wasn't by your side as always.

In the last year, Father got sick, and we had a difficult time. You strengthened, helped, and lifted me so much; how calm I was when you were around. I had enough of your quiet presence by my side. "Mamo," you would say, "the important thing is you being strong." Not sure I thanked you enough for that.

I am glad that in your younger years you experienced a great love, which lasted for five years with your Inbal. You had been built up and had grown together, and already made your plans after the release from the army; everything was so close. God, why?!

My Adi, we were blessed with you as a gift for almost twenty-one years. I thank you for the privilege I was given to be your mother, a child of love, a child of contentment, a child of great light.

You are so alive inside me that I can't say goodbye to you because you will always stay there.

Thank you for what you were, my love. Sorry if I was tough sometimes. I hope that your short life filled you in its way and that you knew happiness in it, as you brought to your father and me.

Yours always from everywhere, I love you an eternal love. Your Mamo

The Little Prince from Squad B
Will no longer see a sheep that eats a flower
And all his roses are thorns now
And his little heart froze like ice

~

Hallel Eizner
My Maya

The last song we heard together this week was "It's Good Now." Of course, as soon as it ended you switched to Mark's set and started dancing.

It was just like that with my Maya. Everything had been so good recently.

I feel that I had gotten to experience our relationship at its best. Almost every conversation ended with the sentence "I love you." We both said it to the other so that there would be no doubt. How good it was together.

There was not a day without us talking or meeting.

When can we go to yoga at Nob's, see the sunset, go jogging, go shopping (because you won't go shopping without me ...)? When can we get coffee, just a long double espresso on ice, please? Just one more.

The last week was particularly magical. We met every chance we had, chatted about everyone. You introduced me to everyone important who I still hadn't met. You had so many friends, and you wanted me to meet them all. You brought me into your world. Step by step so I wouldn't be afraid of how big it was.

My wonderful one, you were at your best—
The most beautiful
The most worthy
The smartest
The happiest
The most loved
You taught me to take it easy, go with the flow, open myself up, try new things, and not limit myself to others.

154

You prepared me for your parties. On our last run you forced me to listen to a set that you liked so that we would be at the same pace. At the end of the run you told me that it bored you, and you moved on to something else. And I stayed with the set because I was afraid to disappoint you.

I was afraid that what we had was too good. I told my mother a month ago that I was afraid. I felt that we were closer than ever, and I was afraid that our friendship would end. She reassured me and said we were friends for life. Sometimes more, sometimes less, but for life.

We fell in love from eighth grade on. We never split up. Even in the army we served together for a while; we couldn't part ways.

During thirteen years of friendship we only fought twice seriously. The first time was over a steak in the freezer. I froze it, you thawed it. And the second time was about a skirt.

From that day forward, we decided not to fight about boys.

You with the fair ones, me with the darker ones.

In our last conversation on Friday, you wrote that you felt beautiful and that you loved me. And I wrote to you that I was happy to have you.

My Maya, my life will not be the same without you. Tel Aviv will not be the same.

The city will be empty without you.

My Maya.

Now, it's not good anymore.

~

Adi Benatiya
The Journey of the Heart

The anticipation,
The butterflies in our stomach before we head out
As we dress
Pack the car
Fuel up
That thrill as if it's our first rave
Yet we feel it every time.
The happiness swelling in our hearts when the music
Floats through the car window
Signaling we're on the right path.
The excitement when we arrive,
Finding the perfect spot to vibe
Exchanging smiles with everyone.
The pure joy of rushing to the dance area
Each finding their spot by a speaker
Or just right in the middle.
And with that, our journey begins
But it never ends.
Smiles, embraces, chats, new friends
Even just through a glance.
Here, everyone's a friend
And there's nothing but love
unconditional love.
The sense of liberation, the elation
That profound joy
A smile so wide
Eyes closed

Hearts overflowing with bliss
Everything that was seen in the night
Transforms in the daylight
And it's always even better.
There's nothing like what the dance floor gives
whether it be the largest or the smallest.
Those who've never experienced it cannot truly comprehend.
The community with love, acceptance, and a strong connection
  to each other
No judgments
No hate
unconditional love
I wish everyone could understand
What I understood
When I first stepped into this world.
And thank you
To those no longer with us, forgive us.
I promise to dance for you,
We'll spread joy and love.
Stir the heavens and the earth
And unite us all
To the truth

~

Becky Riji
Farewell Letter to My Fairy

I finally had the courage to say goodbye to you.

Two days before the Black Saturday, you insisted I come sit with you over a glass of orange juice (only freshly squeezed) in the office so you could have time with Palaya, the new dog I adopted. Without thinking twice I ran out to you. In my wildest dreams I did not think it would be a golden meeting, our last. So thank you for insisting. I was rewarded with a little more of Gabay, because everyone should have a little Gabay in their lives.

I wanted to tell you a few things, because that's what they said to do. You need to talk to someone before you part from them forever . . . They say it helps to process the pain inside . . .

So first, I'm sorry I couldn't stop you from going to the death party, and I'm also sorry I couldn't stop the tears since that Black Saturday, October 7, until we accompanied you on your last journey (you probably laughed at me crying annoyingly like a little girl).

I also wanted to tell you that you left me without my partner in crime, so just know I'll just miss you!

- I'll miss the excitement of waiting for the weekend.
- I'll miss digging into a hamburger at 2 a.m. and then deciding it wasn't enough and getting a knafeh on top of it.
- I'll miss your stories about wacky dates.
- I'll miss dreaming of where we'll travel and when.
- I'll miss every moment of you calling me and saying:

Becky, yaa'la, I feel like leaving everything and going to a Hula-Hoop workshop on some beach. What did I need this residency for?

- I'll miss conversations like, "Becky, leave a key for me, I'm coming to sleep over."
- I'll miss "Gabay, are you coming to the north this weekend? Yaa'la, we're going on a nature hike."
- I'll miss sharing with you our love for animals, and dogs in particular.
- I'll miss deep conversations with you, as well as the shallowest possible about who's good-looking and who's not.
- I'll miss hours of Hula-Hooping, frozen Stella bottles from the stream (or cans if it is at Geula Beach).
- I'll miss your approval for every picture uploaded.
- I'll miss you sleeping over even if you didn't bring clothes for the office for the next day, so then I'd accessorize you and every piece of clothing looked one thousand times better on you than it looked on me.
- I'll miss you helping me plan my birthday for the last three years.
- I'll miss our excitement about the Midburn and at the same time promising each other that "next year we have to get to Burning Man."
- I'll miss you having to add the words "my friend" after every name you mentioned that I wasn't familiar with ... because really, everyone was your friend.

And that's not even a quarter of what I'll miss, because you cannot be explained on a white page.

So Gabay, thank you for everything!

Especially for the little moments when I needed someone to talk to or laugh with or cry with, and it was always you who knocked on the door.

And stop laughing at me up there! Light up your joint that I left on your grave; what are you waiting for?!

I want you to be sure I'll keep smiling, laughing, and dancing at nature raves as if there's no tomorrow, just like you would want. Also be sure that I'll keep being there for your family, and for Boof, Nella, and Alphi when needed. You don't know how much I love them! And what a special connection was created thanks to you! (Especially Grandfather Abraham, who promised a "Mano Shipping" hat . . . you would probably lose it laughing, just seeing this . . .).

Know that I always said you are a fairy in this world, but now you've been upgraded, given big white wings that have turned you into a white angel.

I love you forever and for eternity, Shenshen, mine and so many other beautiful people's.

P.S. I demolished a hamburger before your funeral; you would have been so proud of me!

Rest in peace, my upgraded fairy with wings.

Yours,

Becks

~

David Berdich
My Best Friend Is Gone

This statement presents several challenges:

The challenge in our collective experience as a nation of grappling with the extent of the horrors we are gradually uncovering. The difficulty is coming to terms with, and humbly acknowledging, the fact that our personal loss is merely a fragment of a horrific larger picture. I believe there isn't a citizen in Israel who hasn't felt a personal loss, a direct or indirect consequence of recent events.

The challenge of offering support and comfort, and being there for dear Yuval and the Ben Moshe family. Almost all members of the Hetz squad have been active in various sectors for several days, continuing Ariel's work and legacy.

A constant sense of weakness, each time your picture appears on my phone screen, on a shirt, or simply in a fleeting thought. One of the lesser challenges is selecting the right image to share. In my gallery, spanning the last thirteen years, there are few photos where you aren't present in some way—be it standing next to me, behind the camera, or simply being there in the scene. I had the privilege of experiencing and evolving alongside you during the most defining years of my life, a privilege for which I am immensely grateful.

You were larger than life, a source of admiration for many. Good, pure, and almost too wonderful to be real.

The greatest challenge is coming to terms with what happened.

It will take a long time to understand and process this information, if it's ever possible. Until then, we must remain focused. We are in the midst of a struggle for our home, our humanity, and our values as a nation. It is our duty to complete what you started. We will carry out our task successfully—and we will prevail.

I love you, my dear brother. Shine some light on us from above.

~

The Zionist Leadership Fund
Captain Eden Nemri

Captain Eden Nemri, twenty-two years old, from Modi'in: Eden Nemri, a distinguished swimmer and a member of Israel's youth swimming team, represented the ideal of an exceptional athlete. However, she chose a path of significant military service and enrolled in flying school.

After leaving the course, she volunteered for an elite unit in unmanned aircraft operations, known as the Sky Rider unit, which specializes in gathering operational intelligence.

She served as a combat soldier and later as an officer, taking on the role of team commander. Her team of soldiers regarded her as an exemplary officer—competitive yet caring, deeply committed to her service and unit. She was notably intelligent, knowledgeable, embodied good values, and was a professional par excellence, a true representation of "beautiful Israel."

On the Shabbat of Simchat Torah, at 7 a.m., soldiers in Nahal Oz's women's barracks were awakened by bombardment on the post. The observation soldiers, not being combat soldiers, were unarmed. Eden and her four combat soldiers, along with the others, hurried into the secured shelter with their personal arms.

Soon, a battle erupted close to the shelter where they were crowded together. The post alarm escalated from a "Color Red" alert to a "raid, raid" alert. Inside, Eden made eye contact with her combat unit, then loaded her weapon. Her soldiers followed suit, a decision that, in retrospect, changed the battle's outcome.

The shelter had two exits. Eden, who instinctively took charge as the battle commander of the shelter, guarded the left exit and directed another soldier to secure the right one. The first terrorist tried to enter through the right entrance but was shot and killed by Eden's soldiers.

Realizing the terrorists would likely attempt the left entrance next, Eden decided to hold them off there, providing a chance for the observer soldiers to escape through the now-free right exit.

A group of terrorists, firing and throwing grenades, stormed the opening guarded by Eden. They were met with effective counterfire. These crucial moments, amidst smoke and Eden's brave effort, allowed six observation soldiers and four of her combat soldiers to retreat to the barracks, in which they barricaded themselves until being rescued by paratroopers and Maglan fighters.

Captain Eden Nemri was killed in battle, heroically saving ten Israeli soldiers—six observers and four combat soldiers who were very dear to her.

◆ ◆ ◆

The phrase "The fallen walk first" was coined about ninety years ago by Haim Shturman. A man from Emek Yizrael, he made this statement in memory of his friend Moshe Rosenfeld, who was killed by a group from At-El-Din-El-Kasam during a pursuit. This saying also applies to the women who have fallen; tragically, it is often the best among us who are taken too soon.

In her memory.

~

Guy Polat
In the Place where Humanity Ended— There Was Camille

Camille is a migrant worker who came to Israel from the Philippines five years ago to take care of Nitza, ninety-five years old, from Kibbutz Nirim.

Like everyone else, she got up on the morning of October 7 to the sound of heavy gunfire, and she locked herself up with Nitza in the safe room.

Before eight in the morning, she heard people talking outside the house, and Camille, who had previously also worked in Dubai, realized very quickly that the people outside were not Hebrew-speaking soldiers, but Arabic-speaking terrorists.

She tried to close the safe room's window—but couldn't.

And suddenly—there she was in front of the terrorists. She was supposed to fly two days later to the Philippines to visit her son, and for that she had 1,500 NIS in her wallet that she planned to bring home to the family.

Without thinking twice, she gave the terrorists her wallet and told them: take everything, just don't take the plane ticket from me. She is elderly and does not understand anything. Take everything—and go.

The terrorists took Camille's money—and left.

Then Camille got into bed with Nitza—and hugged her for two and a half hours until the IDF soldiers came to rescue them.

In the meantime, she canceled the plane ticket for the family vacation she had planned. She said: I promised Nitza then that I would not leave her until she died—and I will not.

Of all the heartbreaking stories, I have a special place for all those foreign workers—people from the poorest nations—those who, in order to make a living, flew thousands of kilometers away from home to work in the most difficult and exhausting jobs. Those who collect shekel for shekel in order to send home a few shekels.

And those who somehow got into a conflict in a language and a place they don't understand. And yet, when evil broke out and barbarism took over—they chose to be human.

Like Camille.

~

Liza Kudri
White Lie

I am also the wife of a . . .

No no, my husband wasn't called up for reserve duty due to the situation. He isn't a career soldier shuttled north, south, or engaged in distant operations. Nor is he an enlisted soldier, the child of the entire State of Israel, for whom everyone mobilizes to provide food, clothing, and treats, reflecting the spirit of the Israeli people—to unite in times of crisis.

I am the wife of a policeman. Yes, the one in the blue uniform.

So, you can relax; my husband wasn't called up to reserve duty. Since Black Saturday, he's been working at least twelve-hour shifts, collapsing into bed only to rise for another grueling twelve-hour shift.

Yes yes, take a breath, my children are fine. They just ask every day where daddy is, crying because they miss him. In a desperate bid to soothe them, I lie, saying he'll be home tomorrow to play, but that's a white lie—he'll return, but long after they've cried themselves to sleep.

And no, I don't need offers of help. This isn't temporary for me. My routine, and that of thirty thousand other women, is always like this—during every protest, every US presidential visit, every Independence Day, and countless other occasions that demand police officers work longer, sometimes without days off and for inhumanely long hours.

There's no need for flowers or challah for Shabbat. Celebrating Shabbats, holidays, birthdays, and events alone is routine. It's something we've grown accustomed to.

But there is something you can do: remember the strength of the Israeli Police, how much they sacrifice for the system's efficiency and the safety of all citizens of Israel. Remember this not only now but always. Give us the strength to keep juggling work, home, and children—a perpetual struggle to establish a routine as cops' wives. Give us strength, so we know it's worthwhile, that it's not for naught.

The only thing I ask is for him and all his colleagues to return home safely, weary and worn, but to come back feeling valued and appreciated.

~

Shaked Peretz
What You Are—Remains with Me

My Razi, my life, my dear cousin, my neighbor,

How fortunate it is that we don't get to choose our family. For twenty-three years, I had the privilege of knowing and admiring a remarkable person like you. Thank you for this gift.

Raz, thinking of you fills me with joy and brings a smile to my face. You had such a zest for life, a genuine love for making people happy—a passion you even turned into your profession.

I remember Raz the warrior, your numerous struggles, and how, against all odds, you never gave up. You were resilient to the very end, fighting for life, as surrender was never a part of your lexicon.

Every encounter with you and Shlomi was a recollection of positive experiences from the army, reflecting your optimistic nature.

The last Sukkot holiday we celebrated together as a family was the most memorable and joyful. We stayed up late, playing games, unknowingly bidding you farewell.

On the morning of Saturday, October 7, 2023, strangers desecrated the temple, the Holy of Holies. Raz and his friends faced pure evil.

Raz took command at the outpost, engaging in combat to protect his friends. He led bravely from the bunker, returning fire, neutralizing several terrorists, and saving the lives of his comrades. Raz, the hero at the forefront, encountered terrorists from another direction and was fatally wounded. Raz, who had just saved lives, tragically lost his own.

For fifty-six hours, we turned over every stone for a sign of you, setting up a situation room, praying, pleading for your safe return, united in our concern for Raz.

On Monday, October 9, 2023, at 3:15 p.m., the casualty officers arrived. We never imagined this tragedy would befall us, but it did.

Our dear Razi, we all love you so much, are always proud of you. You died protecting Hashem's name. You were beloved, a man people cherished being around. We are grateful for every day, week, month, and year we spent with you.

Today, we stand, heads bowed, accepting the decree, cherishing who you were, proud of you, loving you, missing you.

The family stands with your parents, your brothers, your Noam, they will walk in your footsteps, remain undefeated—just like you.

We have a hole in our hearts shaped in your image, Raz. It's a painful yet stirring reminder, full of life and joy.

Rest in peace.

God gave, God took, blessed be the name of God.

~

Naomi Hirshfeld
Testimony from Kfar Aza

6:30 Shabbat morning

Heavy artillery fire in the area

Kobi and I jump from bed, run to the window and see the
  unusual number of artillery fire launches, surprised.

We hear a strange unfamiliar noise near us.

Snipers?

Not clear.

Kobi starts making coffee,

Yalla we began another round . . .

That's what we thought . . .

Oh my . . . how wrong we were.

Looking from the window

A white pickup truck stops in the entrance of the
  neighborhood, ten terrorists (maybe more)

Dressed in black masks and rifles

Unloading equipment

Splitting up

Five run on the grass towards our house

five run towards our beloved neighbors

I still have no idea, asking Kobi:

What is this?

Kobi doesn't understand what he sees either.

7:02

A WhatsApp message in the Kfar Aza women's group:

"We have a gang here in the neighborhood shooting guns."

Someone answers:

It's our soldiers.

Another writes:

Get into the safe room.

The terrorists are just a breath away from the house.

I see the white band tied around their heads.

Hamas.

Shouts

Itbach el Yahud

Allahu Akbar

Run to the safe room.

Someone writes: terrorist infiltration

Someone answers: don't cause panic just because

In those two minutes, we still didn't understand, unimaginable innocence.

Life as we knew it was gone.

Very fast, the WhatsApp was filled with cries for help from every corner of the Kibbutz:

They're shooting at the house!

They're here!

They're at my house please help!

Heavy shooting at my house.

Mine too.

We are breached!!!!!! Help please!!!!

8:58 a report of an injured person near the Michlol

Urgent rescue is needed

I send a message to the emergency response unit:

An injured person near the Michlol, tourniquet urgent.

Trying to open the safe room door

Hold the knob tight

Urgently get to my parents

Did someone see/hear Gila Peled her family in the moshav is worried. (Killed in cold blood).

Tamar Kutz, Aviv's mother, writes: "There is no contact with

Aviv Kutz, we need help to check what's happening there."
(Killed in cold blood).
Someone explains how to create a tourniquet
Someone begs please go see what's happening with my parents
Long hours of WhatsApp groups, calls for help, begging,
    locations,
locations of fighters.
In one apartment Ofir Israel and Itay my grandchild.
In another in the young neighborhood, Inbar and his partner
    Adi.
Under our bed in the safe room Oriani.
There are bursts of gunfire in the neighborhood,
Continuous bursts of gunshots, from close by,
From far away,
From everywhere,
I hear shouts,
From a wounded person near the house,
And quiet.
10:18
Inbar writes
Urgent extraction
They're here
Please . . .
And that's it.
All communication is lost with Inbar
All communication lost with all the young residents
I write to Emily
(a classmate of Inbar, lives close to me)
No response.
Itay screams Ofir begs to be let out
I'm hopeless

173

Kobi patrols the house

A terrorist with an MAG walks the paths outside the house

The blinds are shut, the doors are locked.

Silence

Don't talk

Don't breathe

They're here.

Shooting the house

From every direction

Gunfire bursts

The windows shatter

Inbar doesn't answer

The Duvdevan Unit reaches the Kibbutz.

I think

Okay

That's it, It's over.

It's not.

This Holocaust, this massacre, this major disaster that I can't
even start to understand

It's not over

More and more select forces arrive at the Kibbutz

Maglan Duvdevan Paratrooper Navy Seals Givati

More reports of injuries.

More

And more and more

Time passes

And all I can think about is

My Inbar and Adi are gone.

Keep them out of Ofir and Israel

Please Itay stop crying

Please let us hold on

Please don't kill me
Because who will take care of the rest
Please don't kill Kobi
Because who will be my anchor
Please don't kill Oriani
Because I'll die of sorrow
Please don't let the night come
Please make it stop
Our army is strong
19:08
They're here again
The house is surrounded
Heavy shooting at the house
Shouts in Arabic
Oriani is under the bed
The fear is giving me diarrhea
My Kobi the hero
Tries to take apart the door's knob from outside
So we're
Locked from the inside.
He fails.
I see how our lives are running out.
23:00
Thank God Israel Ofir and Itay are rescued.
I hold hope.
0:30
Terrorists on the roof.
I write in the WhatsApp group:
"We have movement on the roof.
It's urgent they're trying to breach.
they're on the roof.

trying to get in."

Strong knocks on the walls.

From every direction.

A few minutes later, a force from Givati arrives, fire exchange.

Strong knocks on the door.

Kobi says: Is it IDF?

We try and listen through the safe room door.

Can't recognize.

Is it soldiers?

Or terrorists trying to get in?

A window is broken.

Glass shattering.

They're at the door.

Saying

IDF IDF.

Kobi whispers: I'm opening.

I said: No, terrorists, don't open.

Kobi makes a decision.

Opens the door that was closed for eighteen hours.

We see soldiers in front of us.

We find it hard to believe.

Two minutes to take our important items.

Get in the Hummer.

Protecting us from every direction.

Pass through the gate.

Arrive at the Alonit convenience store.

Several of our people are there.

I can't breathe.

I burst into tears.

Someone hugs me.

A soldier brings us something to drink.

My legs buckle over.

I'm shaking.

I sit down on the pavement.

The nightmare is not over yet.

It's only beginning.

More and more bitter notifications of dear friends of ours that
were murdered in cold blood, missing.

We pray.

For miracles.

How do we get up from the horrible loss.

How can we continue from here.

Where is my Inbar? Where is Adi?

Maybe they're wounded and can't be reached? Maybe they
were abducted?

I write to my Inbar.

That I love him and to be strong.

No blue checkmark.

No checkmark.

Sunday 12:30 noon.

Unidentified call.

Adi is on the line:

Neomi, we've been saved, we're okay.

I break down.

They suffered thirty hours of agony and their unbelievable
story, an unimaginable miracle,

I'll write about someday.

Thank you to everyone for the support and help,

I'm sorry I'm not returning calls or answering.

I'm still trying to breathe.

~

Nitay Ben Moshe
The Path Has Not Ended

Ariel, you would be proud of me for my matter-of-fact response after Yaron informed me that you were killed, and after I informed Mother, Father, and brothers. You always referred to me as pragmatic, the pragmatic-like brother, and that's how I was. Pragmatic.

Then I found myself sitting alone in an amusement park in New Jersey in the middle of the night, in silence, and just thinking, what a shame, what a waste, what a loss, not for me, not for the family, and not even for my mother—for the country.

You were supposed to be the one who made things right, the one who did things differently, the one who would be followed. You were supposed to do more, make more things right. What a bummer.

More than a month has passed, and I still can't come to terms with the fact that you're not here, maybe because it's natural to me that there's a war, so maybe I don't hear from you because you're busy, and maybe because you're just not dead as far as I'm concerned. Your image isn't dead, what you stand for isn't dead, you're not dead.

You're just not here physically. I just won't see you anymore, I won't talk to you anymore, I won't hear about your accomplishments, but what you inspired, in me, anyway, is so alive and kicking that it's difficult to think that you are no longer.

Having the privilege of being your brother makes me so proud. I am so glad that I had the privilege of being your brother. You were something else, you were just too good to be real, inhuman, yet human.

It is impossible to sum you up and eulogize you. It seems

like something unimaginable to me. You are always with me, Ariel. I love you so much and it hurts me so much, a pain that I never thought I could experience in my life, but your upbringing, and your path: it pains me that it was stopped. It is also the thing that will lift me up.

You once told me that the most beautiful sentence written in a song is—

"Bundle me in sheaves."

So now, I'll have to collect my broken parts and combine them into something worthy of calling—Ariel's brother, what responsibilities you left me, us—the brothers.

Like everything else you've done, your death has added value, and like everything else, you excel in this as well.

Thank you, Ariel, thank you, my brother, thank you, my inspiration. Thank you for what you are to me, not for what you were or for what you will be, but for what you will always remain.

I love you.

~

Netanel Alinson
The War on Humanity

These days, I find myself without words.

I was called to report for reserve duty on Saturday, and since then, like every home in Israel, there has been a lot of activity.

One hundred thirty percent report to duty, with combat soldiers arriving from across the globe. No words.

No words.

This is, of course, a fight for existence, but it is much more.

A war over humanity's nature, over the divine in mankind.

This Shabbat, we read from Genesis one of the most profound contributions of the people of Israel to the world: "And God created man in His own image, in the image of God He created him."

In contrast to ancient nations' myths, where kings are born of mythical gods and commoners from refuse or other unsavory remnants, Israel's key innovation is the belief that human beings, in their essence, possess celestial, heavenly, and sublime qualities.

Yet, right after this, Cain murders Abel and, with his bare hands, annihilates his humanity. The interpretation is that "he saw his brother as an animal," degrading himself to a beast and even lower.

Since then, these two pivotal narratives have formed our foundation:

The belief that humanity can and should aspire to be exemplary, elevated above all.

And alongside it, the understanding that humans can lose their essence and sink lower than animals.

This week we encountered the descendants of murderous Cain, destroyers of creation.

And that's what we're fighting for.

That, and the existence of the only Jewish country in the world, but also for God's essence in humanity.

Let the whole world know.

Condolences,

The battle will be won.

~

Shai Tamir
This is not reality

Those who truly know me understand that
you were my whole life. Those who know me
realize that this is the greatest loss I could ever
face. And those who really knew you are aware
that the world has lost the best there ever was.

Basti, today marks exactly a month since we last spoke. Tomorrow is a month from that horrific Shabbat, from the moment you left my side, and I still can't find the right words to say goodbye.

Is it because there is no God? How can one even begin to summarize? How could you be taken from me, my guardian angel?

My dearest, the difficulties only grow without you, and the hole in my heart does not heal.

You're my soulmate, forever Shai and Adi. Always together, we hoped it would last eternally. So how did it end? How was I left alone? How does one live a life without you?

It feels unreal, like a dream, or rather, a nightmare. I'm waiting for someone to wake me up, to return me to reality, only to realize this is my unfathomable reality.

How can I go on without my best friend? My soul sister, the one who time and again proved that true friendship exists and that I deserve it?

How can life go on without the girl with the infectious laughter? Without the shoulder always ready for my tears? Without the greatest support? Without the honesty and purest heart?

How can I continue without our late-night gossip? Without cruising in the car, screaming our songs aloud? Without our private jokes? Without singing with you, sister? Without dressing the same without planning it? Without our regular get-togethers and conversations that stretched from day to night?

How? Can someone please explain how life can go on without my soulmate?

So, I'll keep asking and hoping to find an answer. And you, rest in peace, my beautiful, and continue to be by my side at every step of my life as you have always been, but this time from above.

My heart screams. Love you forever, my little snail.

~

The Zionist Leadership Fund
Atlanta—Kibbutz Saʾad

Staff Sergeant Rose Lubin,
twenty years old, Kibbutz Saʾad.

Rose was born in Atlanta, Georgia, United States, twenty years ago. At the age of five, following a family trip to Israel, she decided and announced her destiny to make aliyah when she grew up. This decision, her parents recall, influenced every choice she made thereafter. After the next family trip at age six, she refused to go home. By the time she was eight, her parents noticed that she told her friends their friendships would last only until they were eighteen, after which she would leave Atlanta, make aliyah, and enlist in the IDF.

And that's exactly what she did. Two years ago, Rose made aliyah, smoothly integrating into an adoptive family at Kibbutz Saʾad, where she was dearly loved, and realized her dream of enlisting in the Border Police Corps to protect Israel and Jerusalem. Rose, full of energy, happiness, and love, represented Zionism at its very core.

During her basic training graduation, while singing "Hatikva," she burst into tears, overwhelmed with emotion. The morning of Simchat Torah Shabbat, October 7, at her home in Saʾad, located within the Gaza Envelope, her trained instincts immediately kicked in. She quickly grabbed her personal rifle and joined the kibbutz emergency response unit, taking responsibility for securing the entrance gate. She bravely defended the kibbutz, situated just a short run from Kfar Aza, until the evening.

Tragically, on November 6, Rose was killed in action in the Old City of Jerusalem, after bravely confronting a young terrorist who fatally stabbed her.

Thousands of Israelis, nearly all of whom didn't know her personally, attended her funeral, a testament to their respect for her. "The love and enormous support we received from the Israeli public during Rose's Shiva," her parents remarked with a bittersweet smile, "left the boxes of 'Klonex' we brought unopened."

In her memory.

~

Amir Barkol
Drinking Coffee with Him

My request is a little strange, but I would really appreciate your cooperation and sharing. Every day, precisely at 15:00, Sasha Tropnov would insist that his entire Amazon work team leave their keyboards and workstations to join him for coffee. This ritual was sacred to him, and everyone, including Daniel, his supervisor Ilan, and others, would comply. However, for the past month, that charming young man, a real super engineer, hasn't been seen at the 15:00 coffee break. He is in Hamas captivity, along with his mother, grandmother, and girlfriend—essentially his entire family in Israel.

Over the past week, I've had the chance to talk a lot with Sasha's teammates. They remain optimistic about his return, but they express concern that since his entire family is with him in captivity, there is no one in Israel actively thinking about him. They believe that when the awaited day of his return to Israel and to work arrives, it will be important to show him that people did care and think about him.

So, here is my request: Please, at 15:00 today, take a moment to have a cup of coffee, think about Sasha and his family, and then immediately upload a post or story with a picture of your cup of coffee (or of yourself) using the hashtag #coffeeat3withSasha. Sasha's teammates and I will collect these posts with the help of the hashtag, and we plan to show him the pictures one by one the moment he returns home. I promise. Thank you.

~

David Rotman
The Story of Gali Tarshansky

Gali has reached eighth grade at Nofei Habsor, and she can't stand math.

Sports are a different story. She loves them, especially volleyball. She's a champion and plays for the Hapoel Eshkol girls' team.

Whenever she enters a house, classroom, or room, you can't miss her. The decibels rise, as does the mood. It's impossible to rest or remain indifferent when she's around. We must admit, sometimes it can be exhausting . . .

Oh yes, and then there's her love for animals. She can't let any animal pass by without giving it a pet, a hug, or playtime. How many girls do you know who dream of starting a farm for abandoned dogs?

We haven't even mentioned TikTok, or the new makeup corner she set up at home. And let's not forget about mother Reuma, father Ilya, the grandparents, aunts, and uncles.

We also haven't written about her leap from the window of the safe room in a burning house. About trying to escape with the little air left in her lungs. About the agonizing wait to know what had happened to her. And the comforting, yet shocking news that she's alive but held captive by the cruelest of people.

Yet, even in such situations, she manages to make us smile.

You will return, Gali. We know this for certain. There is no other option. Everyone here is waiting for you, and you'll have a new makeup corner. We'll share with you, in pain, the news about your brother Lior and David Noi. We won't stop hugging you. You will achieve all your dreams, Gali.

And it will be soon. We won't let them prolong our agony.
We promise you, Gali.
Promise.

Gali was released as part of a hostage-prisoner exchange between Israel and Hamas in November 2023.

~

Shaked Dimni

Her Life Was Cut Short before Her Time But Is Now Filled with Music, Light and Unending Love

My Rotem, my glorious sun. I have longed to write to you, but I could not bear the feeling of giving up on you. You never gave up on me.

What is my life worth without you, my beautiful child?

Every second that passes is agony, marked by the thought that I will continue to breathe while you are no longer here.

I want to thank you, for the endless hours spent unraveling the mystery of who I am, hours we didn't realize would be so precious. You taught me tenderness, sensitivity, and boundless honesty. Foolishly, it took me too long to comprehend, yet you stood by with a patience that was uniquely yours.

Thank you for the experiences, the privilege of traveling together, listening, dancing at every opportunity, and for our big hugs at every event because we both knew we had each other.

We joked that if we didn't fall in love soon, we would marry, because where else could one find a perfect relationship like ours?

Now, I don't have you anymore. I'm left alone to face life's challenges, the disappointments of love, the peeling walls in our apartment, the empty refrigerator—all the things you used to take care of.

Sometimes, I would sit and watch you, admiring how beautiful and talented you are, how loved, respected, and admired by many. The past few days were impossible, with so many people worried and wishing you well. You were incredible, touching many lives and adding color to their existence.

I long for one more embrace, my Rotem. I didn't know our last hug was just that, and it still wasn't enough for me. Yet, even a hundred years by your side wouldn't have been enough.

In your final moments, I hope we were all on your mind. You always surprised me with your strength and resilience. I hope you remained strong until the end. It breaks my heart to know I wasn't there. How did I let you go alone? You never went anywhere without me.

I wish the whole world could know, Rotem,

That there will never be another like you.

And here I am, not even half a person without you,

Without oxygen, without light,

No color, no beautiful music in my ears.

Everything has become empty, a mere illusion.

May you rest in peace, my dearest friend, the one my soul loved.

I always imagined this song at my chuppah, but you were the greatest love of all.

I'm going out to fight for you and will not return until we prevail.

~

Ofir Galina
Gili's Birthday

Dear Gilad,

Sadly and very late, I wish you a happy birthday!

I hope that in the first month of your new year, you had a chance to taste and touch a little bit of all the good things that the coming year will bring to your doorstep.

Even from afar, somewhere in the Far East, I'm certain that you illuminate everything you choose to touch. I'm overjoyed that you've found a new place to grow and spread your incredible passion for people, for taking action, for pure, simple joy, in the way only you can, with your entire being.

Enjoy your own space in the role that fits you perfectly, and the ability to educate with all your heart, work with all your soul and all your strength, yet still find time in the day to celebrate and forget all your worries.

You're destined for greatness.

I love you and miss you from afar,

Galina

This is what I should have remembered and written to you, from Pai or Rishikesh, because I'm so flaky that I obviously sent a group birthday wish and forgot to congratulate you personally. But with you, it's different. You shine brightly in my life, uplifting me with your presence without needing words.

Ours is a friendship that requires no explanations, where differences blur into similarities, and hearts join in joy without reason.

Gilli, I miss you.

I'll be waiting for you on my balcony when I return.

Unrelated, you are already a bit stoned, just the right amount (it shows in your eyelids).

For our morning coffee, when we breathe in the air of home, you simplify things for me, and I complicate them for you, making everything more complete and easier to bear.

But now, it's not easy for me.

I try to imagine how you would simplify it for me,

Saying that what is, is all there is,

That in your absence, life must still be lived to its fullest.

That we should party, get drunk, and smoke, because life is short and free of excuses.

You'd insist on regular coffee drives and beach visits to maintain your tan and the color of our souls from our travels.

And it hurts.

It will continue to hurt.

Yes, you'd say not everything is perfect, and we shouldn't live in illusions.

The pain will never cease.

You will always be missed.

I wish you could return.

I wish we could sit on the balcony endlessly.

I still can't believe you're not here.

That we'll never meet again.

That the end is already behind us.

Now, you are an eternal memory of who you were,

Instead of just being here.

Please, just be here.
The emptiness is vast.
There's a short circuit in my brain,
And a burning chasm in my heart.
It's not frozen,
But burning.
Come back.
Please.
Don't leave us to face the impossible.
Just come back.

~

The Mangedi Family
Dor, Our Brother, the Heart of Our Home

We can't believe we have to speak of you in the past tense, struggling to comprehend this surreal situation we've been forced into. It is impossible to describe the magnitude of the void in our family's hearts.

You were the light of our home, its voice, its wind, its hustle and bustle. Always present for each and every brother, through countless hours, days, and nights. Your heart was huge, filled with generosity and action. There was nothing we needed that you didn't provide.

You were everyone's helper, caregiver, and supporter. Whenever someone needed you, you would appear, declaring, "Dor the King has arrived," and we would all laugh. We were your biggest fans, always boasting to others, "Want to see our brother?" The most handsome in the world. There was nobody like you, and there will never be anyone like you again. You were unique in this world, truly irreplaceable.

Thank you for being our guardian, our protective shield, sacrificing yourself so we could live with dignity and without fear, even though now we bear an unhealable hole in our hearts.

You were the best police officer and warrior, a true hero, the boy with the largest heart, the most special of friends, the magic in our world.

As hours and days pass, we are crumbling.

We endured nine agonizing days of uncertainty, weeping, aching, and praying for your return. Clinging to every shred of hope, every glimmer of light.

Since that Saturday, we waited for you at the door, day and night merging into an eternity.

You were righteous, taken from us by the hands of evil on a day we'll never forget, October 7, 2023, 22 Tishrei Tashpad, Simchat Torah. You were laid to rest on Rosh Chodesh Cheshvan.

That fateful morning, you leapt from bed, exclaiming, "Mother, war," quickly organizing and heading south.

By 14:13, you were unreachable, and despite our attempts to reassure Mom, a mother's heart knows.

Mother misses you desperately. Unable to bear this immense pain, she collapses.

We strive to stay strong for her, never leaving her side. We know how much she meant to you, and we honor your will to protect and prevail.

The way you died leaves no doubt about your righteousness, your generosity, your sacrifice in battle. We could live a hundred and twenty years as righteous beings and still not reach your level, our king.

You died a martyr's death, a warrior's death, fearlessly defending our country and its people. We are your admirers, cherishing your memory every day, our warrior.

In your death, you have commanded us to live.

We promise to keep our family safe.

We vow to serve our country and its flag in your spirit, to honor your memory in every moment of our lives.

Gradually, our minds begin to grasp this reality, and with understanding comes an ever-intensifying pain. We love you, our brother, blood of our blood. Watch over us from above, grant us strength. We hurt and miss you immensely. Rest in peace, our hero.

We will always remember you forever, brother, and you know we will meet again at the end.

~

Iris Mangedi
The Love of My Life

My child, the love of my life,

On October 7, 2023, the world stopped. You got up quickly, shouting, "Mother, war!" I didn't know that would be the last time I would see you.

My child, my life changed in an instant, became filled with sadness, pain, and endless tears.

Who will call me Memo now?

Who will ask, "Mother, did you eat?"

Who will take care of me?

Who will I call Dor?

I am left in agony, a part of my body, a piece of my heart, taken from me. We were just talking about how I was waiting for your children, how I would spoil them and care for them, a joy I will never experience.

Dori, it's hard for me, so very hard. I am longing for the day we meet again.

I can't believe I can only see you in pictures, not beside me. I have hung your photos all around the house, so we will never forget you.

My Dor, the light in our home has gone out. How do we continue, my child? How?

Who will climb into bed and cuddle with me?

Who will remind me, "Mother, take care of yourself"?

Who will prepare the Shabbat chair for me, making sure it's comfortable, taking care of me, urging, "Mom, eat"?

I'm still at home, sitting on the couch, waiting for you, hoping you might come suddenly, and I'll jump on you like any mother whose son has returned from war.

But you will not come back, my son.

My dear son, you will be engraved in my heart until my last day, my love.

May your memory be a blessing; rest in peace, my child.

I love you the most in the world,

Mom

~

Dana Varon
Fedia

Fedia, can you hear?

With a name like yours, it seems you are ascending to heaven to save God.

It appears that sometimes His holiness needs us to redeem Him from the exile He has sentenced us all to.

Go tell Him that we forgive Him, miss Him, and feel a bit jealous that He has been joined by so many good people. The best, indeed.

Tell Him He has good taste, and that despite being merciful and compassionate, He is also terrible, as it is written: "Great and terrible God, give redemption to Your people." Inform Him that the members of the Knesset fainted, some threw up and cried at the horrific movie of the Gaza Envelope, and most could not endure till the end. And, by the way, ask Him, are we there yet?

At the end. Is this what we have waited for and anticipated for years? Gog and Magog and all that.

Tell Him that we are a nation of heroes and lionesses, seeking mercy and grace. Say that we aren't perfect, but we're still worthy, paying a high price with a bitter taste. And it's strange, that a person with your eyes and a name like "Fedia" is precisely suited for redeeming God from this diaspora.

Below, we have 238 people ready to redeem, updated continuously. It includes babies, elders, soldiers, and women as well. It's truly surreal to think that, because we believed, we have no one else to blame. There's justice, magnified and sanctified, and hope for Beit Hamikdash.

Tell Him, Fedia, that you represent all the living and the dead, and what was, was. But from here forward, this can't continue. Enough. Let the answer be found with love, filled, soaring, containing, building, ruling, and returning them all.

You too, Fedia. He will return with might—tell Him you're His last soldier.

This is how I talk to God, don't be mad. And He loves me like this. The pain is too great to contain. And may He be blessed for all He contains.

~

Mia Schem
I Will Never Forget October 7, 2023.

The pain and the fear, the horrific sights,
the friends who will not return,
And those we need to bring back.
But we will prevail, we will dance!

~

While collecting all these stories we wept and prayed, and most importantly we were filled with hope.

Our reality is so painful; anyone who was not there could never really understand.

It is our privilege to publicize these stories, in their original form, very lightly edited to address errors in translation.

This book was created voluntarily as a mission to commemorate the events of October 7 and the war that followed.

We strongly hope for better days of unity, we pray for the return of all the hostages, and we wish speedy recovery, in body and soul, to all the victims and the survivors.

A big thank you to each and every one of you who contributed to bringing this book to light.

A special thanks to Lily Marks for her special dedication to the project.

Visit our website—Oct7book.com